REASON AND GENIUS:

Studies in Their Origin

REASON AND GENIUS:

STUDIES IN THEIR ORIGIN

By ALFRED HOCK, M.D.

GREENWOOD PRESS, PUBLISHERS
WESTPORT, CONNECTICUT

ACKNOWLEDGMENT

Grateful acknowledgment is made to Mr. John Gutman for his translation of the chapter on Genius and to my wife's numerous and valuable suggestions when the book was being conceived and her patient assistance in its final stages.

Copyright 1960 by Philosophical Library, Inc.

All rights reserved

Originally published in 1960
by Philosophical Library, New York

Reprinted with the permission
of Philosophical Library

First Greenwood Reprinting 1971

Library of Congress Catalogue Card Number 70-138150

ISBN 0-8371-5607-6

Printed in the United States of America

CONTENTS

REASON

INTRODUCTION

Can there be anything more interesting to man than the explanation of himself? Up to now he is still far from the desired clarification.

Not even the important question whether or not he is to be considered a reasonable being permits an uncontradictable answer. Along with examples from history showing that man is capable of the highest mental performance, there are innumerable others which reveal his quite unreasonable behavior.

Because of the absence of comparative statistical data, there is no proof that the percentage of reasonable individuals has increased during the course of history. There are no certain signs that the human race is more reasonable at present than it was in the age of John Stuart Mill, who considered it "a collection of a few wise and many foolish individuals."

But for that purpose we must dig deep into the very beginnings of life and follow it through to its highest manifestations; i.e., we must look for the answer to the question of how life originated in non-living matter, how the cell formed from inorganic matter, how the multicellular—including the human—organism arose from the undifferentiated cell, that is, the unicellular organism, and what enabled the human being to develop his mind: consciousness, fantasy, reason.

How far physical powers are related to what we call *life* and *mind* is still endlessly disputed. Great uncertainty also prevails as to the causes of differences in the physical and moral behavior of different individuals. Many investigators believe there are different — higher and lower — human types. Differences in human behavior are so great that there is hardly any hope of finding a formula for their etiological explanation. However, can we not find in human individuals, as in all physical substances, along with those characteristics in which they differ from one another, those which are common to all?

We have already obtained by abstraction from concrete observations certain general formulations—the Laws of Nature. There is hope that scientific investigation could provide similar symbols that would be useful in acquiring deeper understanding of the human mind in general and reason in particular.

The number of facts related to the subject handled here is so vast that the temptation of writing a voluminous book was great. The author, however, deemed it preferable to compress his statements into a small space because the subject is of interest to a much wider circle of readers than the mere specialist.

Chapter I

1. Different Conceptions of the nature of life phenomena. Building materials and stimulating substances. Vitamines, enzymes, hormones.

Interplay of glands producing these.

No sharp boundary between inert and living matter, between animals, plants and the earth which they inhabit.

2. Origin of life. Views of Darwin, Haldane, Oparin, Johnsen, Urey [1]

The living cell is not the most primitive representative of life. Links between living and nonliving. Precellular stages.

3. Physico-chemical processes in the cell the basis of life. Colloidal substances, proteins, crystalloids, ions, nucleoproteins. Irritants as exciting cause of life processes. Cell function. Irritability. Stability of chemical composition and electric charge of normal cell in the process of "coming into being and of decaying" . . . breakdown and reconstruction. Sleep—a conserver of energy.

4. Cell membrane, Endocrines, nervous psychic stimuli. Arndt-Schulz Law. The ability of living protoplasm to incorporate elementary stimuli. The significance of stimulus-storage for all living processes including the intellect.

5. The nervous system as mediator between milieu and organism.

Reflex mechanism. Effect of stimulus repetition on functions and forms of life. Allergy, Specific energy. Habit. Purposefulness of living being.

6. Attempts toward a mechanistic explanation of life: Lamarck, Darwin, De Vries.

Theory of synthesis (Simpson), Reflections on energy make the necessity of a synthetic theory of life comprehensible.

> *Und doch ist die Welt ein einfach Rad,*
> *in dem ganzen Kreis sich gleich und gleich.*
> *das uns aber so wunderlich vorkommt,*
> *weil wir selbst in ihm herumgetrieben werden.*
>
> Goethe: *Italienische Reise*

> And yet the world is a simple wheel,
> the same everywhere over its entire circumference,
> but it seems so strange to us, because
> we ourselves rotate within it.
>
> Goethe: *Italian Journey*

A long time ago the great research worker Virchov expressed the view that life is only a special kind of motion. According to him, the body may indeed be the bearer of life; its manifestations, however, are but the expression of irritability produced by the movement processes within its substance. Self-stimulation, i.e., stimulation not produced by movement but inherent in the substance, Virchov considered unimaginable.

Already science has made it possible for man to calculate accurately the movement that a definite mechanical force will impart to a given physical body. (Ernst Mach)

It is well known today that chemical, electromagnetic energy and radiation differ from mechanical energy only quantitatively, not qualitatively, and that there is equivalence between mass and energy. In other words, energy can assume widely varying shapes, one form of energy being transmutable into another.

6

This insight suggests the idea that the manifestations of life and mind may be but additional examples of the transformation of one kind of energy into another.

Of course, we are accustomed to look at manifestations of the mind as fundamentally different from those of matter, but because of the great practical and theoretical significance of the answer we get to this question, we cannot renounce inquiring whether these are not but special aspects of Nature, i.e., both of the same essence.

Many scientists are rejecting this theory and are explaining life phenomena by a special vital force innate in every single individual, having its goal in itself (entelechy). According to them, only living matter possesses the ability to synthesize lower elements of form into higher units—tissues, organs, and partial functions into more complicated, purposeful ones. Such a struggle toward a goal is no better explained without a preliminary plan, i.e., mechanically, than the origin of a melody, a word, reasoned judgment, if explained by purely mechanical arrangements of tones, letters and words. These scientists doubt that a specific pattern of behavior could emerge from the interplay of minimal favorable variations and accumulations of separate elements entirely wanting any purpose or teleological character.

August Bier once wrote: "The causality of the living thing is not blind like lifeless nature. The psyche behaves like a person with a purpose, i.e., the crow immediately scents an enemy in the eagle owl even when seeing it for the first time. The songbird sings the song of its species even though, having been artifically incubated, it has had no chance of hearing it before.[2] The bird of passage leaves its home before the threat of famine."

Reactions which follow the removal of a piece of skin show all the tendency for recovery. Penetration of toxins and bacteria into the organism induces the immigration of leucocytes into the blood and the production of antitoxins adapted for the destruction of the bacteria. The organism reacts to every failure of function with efforts for its restoration.

In short, the biologists and psychologists known as "holists" or "neovitalists" consider the behavior of the organism, in contrast with that of a mechanical automaton, to be directed by a purposeful perception structure. The parts of this structure, by participating in the composition of the organism, contribute toward better adaptation of the organism to its goal. The configuration of mental processes is never to be explained entirely by mechanistic interpretation, i.e., as merely the sum of its parts. A mental function—the so called "Gestalt"—has never yet been observed to arise by incorporation of elementary stimuli. All of its parts are related to the outcome of the struggle toward the goal from the very beginning, it is a conditioned "closed structure" (Burkamp). It has "concrete entirety characteristics with internal regularities, and a characteristic entirety with changes of the parts." (Wertheimer).

Hale's discovery in 1727 that the movement of sap in the living plant takes place in the same way as it does in nonorganic porous bodies, indicated that the processes to which living phenomena owe their origin are basically the same as the simplest chemical reactions.

That life phenomena are to be considered processes of energy can no longer be disputed. Intake of food by the organism is nothing but metabolism with production of energy in the form of heat. The state of the mature cell is due to the synthetic and retrograde reactions proceeding at equal rates of speed. Both are merely the effects produced by the interplay of physical and chemical laws.[3] Every action can be explained in "the terms of its antecedents." "Life is fundamentally a product of catalytic laws in colloidal systems of matter throughout long periods of geologic time."[4]

Food, to have full nutrient value, must contain in addition to the necessary building substances—in an

8

amount not below the physiological minimum—supplementary and stimulating substances, vitamins, indispensable for the vital functions. These are contained in the yolk of the egg, in fish, codliver oil, in fruit such as oranges, lemons, tomatoes, and in vegetables and meat. Deficiency of vitamins gives rise to serious diseases.[5]

Other extremely sensitive substances with specific effects, the hormones, are produced by the tiny endocrine glands scattered over the human body. These "interact with one another and powerfully modify the character and functions of the living body" in such a way that a fraction of a milligram of the effective substance can raise the tension in a far distant organ. Some of these substances, prolan a and b, are produced in increasing amounts in the anterior lobe of the cerebral appendage, the hypophysis, as soon as the sex glands notify it of a deficiency. Another, insulin, is indispensable for the metabolism of sugar in the body. The absence of the suprarenal hormone, cortin, produces a high degree of fatigue, even exhaustion. The thyroid plays a fundamental role in the regulation of body growth and body heat and influences bone development. Its chief function is the increase of the oxidative processes.

Each substance secreted by an endocrine gland exercises an effect on the other glands. Often several of them affect the same life function which contributes to the security of the organism. Of extremely great significance seems to be the interplay between the hypothalamus and the anterior pituitary,[6] the gland lying at the base of the brain. A pathologically increased activity of the *pars anterior* (anterior part) of the hypophysis, the so called hyperpituitarism, expresses itself as overgrowth . . . gigantism . . . when originating in youth; acromegaly when it originates in adult. The diminished activity expresses itself as an excessive, often rapid deposition of fat with persistence of infantile sexual characteristics, when the process dates from youth and a tendency toward

9

loss of the required signs of adolescence when it appears in adult life."

The variety of effects due to a single substance is demonstrable by the "cyclotrope reaction," which is apparently produced by the suprarenal hormone, adrenalin. The reaction appears when the organism is in need or danger; it manifests itself by increase in blood pressure and respiration and the contraction of the spleen. Its rich supply of blood corpuscles being driven into the body, an increase of oxygen surface and a decrease of muscular fatigue take place.

Another important group of substances produced by the organism are the enzymes which have been described as "natural catalysts producing sudden changes in the chemical order possessing the ability of acting on one chemical to turn it into another without themselves being affected by the process."

With the progress of science ever new interrelationships have been discovered besides those between the different products of the endocrine glands and vitamins and enzymes. Such are the interrelationship between sex hormones and ergosterin, biliary acids and vitamin D. Isopren serves as building stone for India rubber, terpene, camphor and some odoriferous substances. One of these, phytol, is more closely related to chlorophyl, the green in the leaves of plants and to the hemoglobin of animal blood pigment.

Closer observation clearly demonstrates that no sharp boundary exists between inert and living material, nor between the past and the present: "Nitrogen, one of the principal constituents of living matter is consequently transferred from the atmosphere to fixing bacteria in the soil to plants, to animals—including man—and then through the activities of putrefactive bacteria back to the atmosphere the process begins anew."[7]

There is a close relationship between our earth and animals and plants and, in turn, these are closely related

10

to each other. The transition between the two seems to be represented by some lower organisms, such as the different species of viruses.

The more insight was gained into the physico-chemical phenomena of life, the smaller became the cleavage between morphology and chemistry.[8]

Pasteur's attempt to understand life on earth as "the result of germs having been wafted from some undeterminable outside source by the pressure of light,"[9] proved just as elusive as that of Svante Arrhenius. Neither got an answer to the question of: how life has arisen from nonliving matter.

Of course no one has yet been able to show that spontaneous generation does occur and under what conditions life first appeared.

That life originated from the ocean is evident. Unicellular organisms lose their water-content in any other but aqueous environment and die of dehydration. Moreover life can only last in the presence of fresh or sea water. In sea water sodium, calcium and many other inorganic substances are present and in the same concentration as in the body fluids and in the blood. This is important because all living cells are unable to endure more than very slight deviations from the neutrality of their environment. Mere contact with metal salts causes precipitation of albumin which results in disease or death. The narrow zone between the lowest and highest temperature in which living organisms have evolved is the same as the range where enzymes can exist and speed the chemical reactions of metabolism.[10] According to Johnsen: "The first selfduplicating molecules must have been relatively small and simple. Because of their simplicity they were more stable to heat. With the cooling of the earth it became possible for more complex molecules to survive and evolution proceeded in every feasible direction. Out of it has emerged present day life in all its magnificent array. Heat makes it go and heat makes

11

it stop again. Whatever the future holds in store for us rests ultimately on heat and on the compromise between too little and too much."

The most competent investigators—Darwin, Haldane, Oparin[11] have adopted the view that conditions no longer exist today for a "primary origin of life formation from such complex giant molecules as the protein compounds of living substances by transformation from simpler organic and inorganic substances, because living creatures today quickly consume and destroy the supply of organic substances. Only in a primitive ocean of a sterile, lifeless planet, in which the water reaches the consistency of hot molten soup (Haldane), could the first precursors of life find sufficient accumulation of food to enable them, by long continued action, to bring forth life from nonliving material with the aid of enzymes and by the action of ultraviolet light from a mixture of water, ammonia and carbon dioxide."

Recently Harold Urey conceived a new theory of atmospheric changes supported by tests. According to Urey billions of years back the earth atmosphere was highly electrified by countless flashes of lightning. The atmosphere of the infant earth, then made up by methane, ammonia and hydrogen, changed in the course of time into the one we have.[12]

While Virchov still regarded the living cell as the basic element of the plant and animal body and as the most primitive representative of life, it is known today that there are "precellular stages" of development. Just as the limits between animal and plant hormones fade, so do the limits between animals and plants in general. There are plants which have the characteristics usually described to animals. The virus causing the mosaic disease of the tobacco plant reproduces without breathing and without metabolism and, even when converted into a crystalline form,[13] remains infectious. Perhaps such contagia within the cell may be considered the bridge

12

between living and nonliving matter. Their size is so small, as low as 30 billionth of a millimeter, that they cannot be seen with the ultramicroscope. The size can be determined only by means of filters with different-sized pores.

The basis of those physical and chemical processes constituting that which we call "life," is more clearly understood by the study of the cell. Cells consist of colloidal systems made up of solutions of protein in water and lipoids which hold electrolytes in labile form, surrounded by a membrane that varies in permeability."[14] These "colloidally dispersed substances" are most significant as the vital dynamics of living matter of intracellular and extracellular substances. Because of its colloidal structure, protoplasm diffuses with difficulty through parchment, paper and animal substances. In spite of the fact that it consists of 75% water, it is insoluble in it. The molecules may be contained in the solid, liquid and gaseous states side by side. These molecules are larger than those of other substances. The size of their contact-surfaces facilitates the building up as well as the breaking down of the extraordinarily great exchange of energy so necessary for living substances, whereby food, such as sugar etc., is broken down into smaller components. "The entirely different nature of the protein-cell and that of the body fluids offers the basis for activity between the cell and the plasm."

Just as the work-capacity of any other machine, that of the living cell depends on the substances added to it, i.e.: food for the free energy it contains. The constant changes in body-cells by rearrangement of colloids and crystalloids and by osmotic processes produce changes in the permeability of the cell-membrane. The intake and release of electrolytes regulate the function and maintenance of the structure of the organism. The ions —those very small electrically charged particles of atom groups varying in concentration and in sign, and composing the living organism—produce, as in an accumulator, a constant stream of electrical discharges and chemical changes. Every withdrawal of effective energy, by disturbing the ionic equilibrium, changes the bioelectrical tension and thus also the cell function. This action on living substance is called "excitability or irritability." The change of its function is called "life."

As a result of its extraordinary sensitivity to the slightest displacement in the ionic equilibrium and in material composition after every functional requisition, the normal cell strives to restore the used substance. Its chemical composition and electrostatic charges are extraordinarily constant. Not until the lost energy is restored, is it again ready for action. All components of the body are in constant state of decomposition and resynthesis. The dynamic life process goes on unceasingly and with extraordinary rapidity. Nothing is really dead; everywhere life is in the process of coming into being and passing.

For the replacing and restoring of bioelectrical energies consumed during waking hours sleep is indispensable. This is one of its most important functions.

The changes in osmosis, in cell permeability and in electrical potential together with the chemical and physical rearrangement of the colloids and crystalloids to form new aggregates, represent the stimuli which determine cell activity. The actual stimulation depends on the previous signs of the stored electricity and the amount of its excess. Groups of chemical substances of a very complex nature, the "nucleoproteins"—themselves compounded from simpler chemical groups, the amino acids —are the basic building blocks of living matter. The protein we consume in the form of milk, egg etc., we break down into amino acids which afterwards are rebuilt into protein composing all living matter. The molecular size of amino acids and their position on the atomic weight scale are more responsible for all biological peculiarities than their ordinary chemical properties. This also applies to the formation of body tissues and all fundamental life processes, the normal as well as the pathological: ability to fight infection; digestion of food; tissue formation and reproduction of species. (Linus Pauling).

Through the thin membrane which separates the living cell from its environment and also connects it with the environment, the forces of the surrounding world are able to act on the cell and induce reactions within it. The cell-membrane, due to its fat-like envelope—a system of substances called buffer mixtures—cannot be easily penetrated in its resting condition. If, however, the cell is stimulated, then the cell membrane becomes permeable to water, salts, lecithin, cholesterin etc. Whatever has excited it externally or internally is called "stimulus" and the change in its substance the "irritation state." Endocrines, nervous and psychic influences participate as well as specific salts. Calcium is indispensable for the formation of the cell membrane and its maintenance. Sodium favors its dissolution and accordingly increases its permeability.

The logical assumption that the strength of the reaction parallels the strength of the stimulus gave rise to the law: "weak stimuli activate life activity; moderate ones accelerate it, strong ones inhibit it."[15]

The universal validity of this law has been contested with good reason. The conclusion that a stimulus which in a certain dosage has an inhibitory or fatal effect, must have an inciting one in another dosage is refuted as incorrect. An apparent stimulation can also be the result of inhibition. Many facts prove that the law is not generally applicable to physical and mental phenomena. A very slight trauma can set in motion severe unpredictable effects, such as the destruction of the jaw bone in a phosphorous worker; an eruption in a syphilitic; a cancer in an anilin worker. The most insignificant irritation

15

for one person can result in an attack of madness for another; e.g. fright at the sight of a dog or even a mouse. Many nervous people are regularly affected by palpitations of the heart and agoraphobia whenever they come back to the place where they once had been caught by a storm. I. H. Schulz relates the case of a mother who ever since the day she sat in the garden of a hospital anxiously awaiting the result of an operation, for which she had assumed entire responsibility, on her only child suffered from hay fever whenever she smelled a particular blossom. This flower had been blooming in the garden at that time.

On the other hand, an elementary incident or a shattering experience may produce no noticeable effect. Not a single one of a series of young girls who had been the victims of a rape, retained a trace of recollection of this experience six years later.

Moreover, it can be observed that a stimulus, if it is powerful [16] will inhibit another reaction which would otherwise accompany it. An apparent stimulation can also be the result of decreased inhibition. Such an abnormal reflex action could, for example, be experimentally produced in a grass frog as follows: at the moment when the female was embraced and her skin grasped, the male did not respond with the stereotyped jerking of his clasped legs as a defense reaction, but with firmer clasping.

By taking into account the effect of stimuli exerted in the past we get a clearer understanding of the differences in the type of reaction. For instance: "In fish had been observed that the female which usually swims about passively in the water, becomes excited by the continuous love play of the male and finally participates in the play herself, thus doubtless attains an increased state of excitation. . . . Nowhere are such phenomena observed in such great numbers as in the case of birds, where the male by indefatigable love play has actually to exhaust

16

himself until the female has attained such a high degree of sensuality that she yields to the pressure of the male. Indeed, the striking colors and forms of the male, the luring sounds and odors attract the attention of the female and get her excited. However, the entire complex of such sensory impressions need be repeated very often before that degree of sensuality is attained which brings the sexes together." [17]

The same results as those observed in nature can be attained experimentally by the irritation of the spinal root with a single charge of an electrical induction apparatus: the first charge produces no perceptible excitation, but its repetition results in a prolonged tetanic muscle spasm. In general, living protoplasm has the ability to store stimulations; preceding stimuli rendering it more receptive to subsequent ones. The single stimulus signifies only one link in the chain of causative factors.

Semon formalized the ever repeated experience that living matter possesses a memory. His "mnemic law," as he calls it, is formulated as follows: "All similar stimulations leave behind in the organism a coherent engram complex which will, with repetition of only a partial stimulus, induce a visible excitation. The most severe reactions are produced by those stimuli which meet in the living tissue with most of the traces of earlier reactions and not by those stimuli which are the most intensive, as one would be inclined to assume. Intensifying of a stimulus soon approaches a limit which, if exceeded, brings about fatigue and death."

By making the assumption that the same tract of the nervous system containing already traces of older stimuli in form of impressions, is acted upon by a series of new stimuli meeting those left behind, we have no difficulty to understand the variety of functions and forms. In other words: the plasticity of the protoplasm as produced by association and interference of stimuli.

The irritability of infusoria, protozoa, i.e.: single-celled

17

organisms, extends over the entire body and appears uniquely as contractility.

The reaction of multicellular organisms—metazoa—are more complicated. A single mechanical, electrical etc. irritation of the paw of a dog manifests itself by movement of the paw, barking, alteration of breathing etc., i.e. by general reactions. With repetitions of the irritation the paw reflex becomes more and more isolated.

The real inner relationship of the almost limitless variety of manifestations of mental-physical phenomena (feeling, sensation, affect, mood, perception, image, muscle-contraction, glandular secretion, "external plastic behavior") of the multi-cellular organism are concealed from the superficial observer. He finds it difficult to imagine how through stimulus and response certain effects are produced in the living substance by the constantly changing environment. The connection becomes clearer as soon as we realize that previous reactions were necessary to carve the path for the ones which follow.

The space-time relation between simultaneous or shortly successive elementary irritations or between perceived sensations gives us an idea of how the uninterrupted chain of life processes, the involuntary activities of the body and the conscious activities guided by will and intellect were uniformly originated. We get an insight not only into how, from closely related partial processes of the reflex type, the impersonal drives and instincts, such as the flight-movement of the infusoria, the fighting behavior of the ants, the love play of the vineyard snails are formed. This also applies to images like the idea of toxicity or eatability of a mushroom or a berry, or even to abstract concepts, like causality, substance, etc.

In animals possessing a nervous system this system makes possible the conversion of an external motion into an internal one, serving as a transformer suited to transfer the movements arising in the environment to the organ.

18

What appears to the superficial observer as life supplied by vital or specific energy, is, in reality, produced by mechanical, chemical, specific or nonspecific etc. irritations. They are conducted by the peripheral nervous apparatus to the nerve centers, from which the excitation is carried on by way of the centrifugal path to the organs. Since the individual constitution is shaped by the union of egg and semen and is the mere expression of associations of excitations repeated through many generations, it is not surprizing that, as a rule, the reflex-mechanisms are fixed, i.e. limited to the species.

A frequent exception to this rule are the "conditioned reflexes" discovered by Pavlov in 1878. What are these? "A reflex is said to be conditioned if a reflex action normally excited by a stimulus of one kind can be excited by another stimulus through association, for instance, when the flow of saliva due to the presence of food comes to be produced by ringing a bell, the reflex reaction of the salivary gland is said to be conditioned." [18]

The mere sight of a red cloth can set up an extremely severe state of excitation in a bull; the sight of a lamb or just hearing it bleat can start the milk dropping from the udder of the milk-sheep. Dogs can be conditioned by training to take meat only at a definite sound; in the case of any other sound (contrasting tone) they leave it alone.

Experience proves that by bringing together any indifferent stimulus with a specific one we can shape ever new associative reflexes in the degree of setting up new conductions between the peripheral and central receiving nervous apparatus. If a totally nonspecific stimulus, e.g. a trumpet sound, is combined 30-40 times with an injection of a sterile bacterial suspension into the abdominal cavity of an experimental animal, the stimulus of the trumpet sound alone will in the end be sufficient to produce an inflammatory extravasation of fluid in the abdominal cavity such as could have been previously

19

caused by the injection of bacteria. After having injected large doses of morphine for seven days into a dog, on the eighth day a mere touching of the injection site was sufficient to produce the same effect of morphine intoxication. The more excitable the animal was previously, the more sensitive its nervous system, the more rapidly such conditioned reflexes could be developed. Often a single association was sufficient to set up a stable effect.

Experiences such as these enable us to get a glimpse of the previously obscure origin of pathological conditions; to understand, for example, how frequently introduction of the same substance—injection of foreign protein, serum a.s.f.—can render the entire organism hypersensitive. In the "allergic" condition thus produced the organism becomes more resistant to certain toxins and infections.

Perhaps the "specific energy" i.e. the property of the organ to react in the *same* typical predetermined way to various stimuli, can be explained in the same way. According to the type of the stimulus by which the individual cell group had been frequently and repeatedly affected, it was bound to attain a particular sensitivity which failed to affect other cell groups. A gland had thus to acquire the capacity of secreting but not to perceive, a muscle contractility but not the capacity to think, etc.

The force of habit is another form in which the effect of frequent repetition of a stimulus may become manifest —an experience which once suggested to a French explorer the idea of defining life as "getting accustomed."

The attempt to see behind life metaphysical forces like Bergson's "Élan vital" or Driesch's "Entelechy," a nonphysical power that has created the world, directing it according to a plan, had to give way more and more to a mechanistic explanation of evolution. Life as well as the manifold forms of its expression and of the purposefulness of the functions of living beings are viewed as the effect of the interplay of stimuli.

20

Modern science does not view the world as stationary but every organic form as the expression of "a flux of processes, its components in a continuous change." [19] According to the author just quoted science is going to evolve a quantitative theory of growth, a dynamic morphology, i.e. biology attaining the status of an exact science. The capability of calculating the results of the counteraction of anabolism and catabolism of the building material of living creatures may permit us to make quantitative predictions confirmed by experiment.

Of course, the path beginning from the first attempts of explaining evolution mechanistically up to the ideas in vogue at the present time has been a long one. Lamarck, the first to be concerned with explaining in detail the origin of variation and the ever increasing complexity of organization, made the assumption that this development was caused by adaptation in function and form to changing environment without any selection. Lamarck looked at the multiplicity of living nature as resulting from individual adaptation which, once set in motion, became fixed in the course of many generations.

There are many adherents to the theory that an organ disappears if permanently put out of use and that, on the other hand, the lasting need for a new characteristic tends to give rise to the development of new habits, usages and organs, for instance, the need of insects for protective coloration. [20]

This conception seemed to be supported by: *ad a*) Experiments with barley, maize, snap dragon, the fruit fly drosophila, mice and others. They seem to show that mutations are not only produced by the action of radium, X-rays, high temperatures and toxins such as alcohol, mercury, iodine and arsenic, but are handed down for many generations. Malformed offsprings of mice crossed with normal mice inherited the characteristics according to Mendelian laws. The off-spring of mice which had

21

been trained to feed at the sign of a certain bell needed a considerably shorter period for training.[21] Crossings in human beings which could be used as proof have not yet been attempted, because homo sapiens develops very slowly and because the number of offsprings of each human pair is restricted. *ad b) Observations of nature.* Without any training and without ever having seen the rescue of an unfortunate individual, a Saint Bernard dog is able to carry out all the details of a rescue in a given case, although such training in his forbears has begun only 250 years ago.[22] The mutation of music appreciation has developed during recent centuries by progressive cerebration as emphasized by Economo,[23] since the ancients perceived only rhythm.

The great significance of remixing of chromosomes and genes as bearers of hereditary characteristics is not prejudicial to the idea that the environment by perpetually changing the sum total of hereditary endowment can bring about the acquisition or loss of characteristics. Ramon y Cajal[24] believes "the effect of environmental factors on heredity can no longer be contested."

According to the views of most investigators today, all the proofs favoring these theories are in part erroneous and in part to be better explained in another way. "The concept of lamarckism appears to be definitively exploded. . . . even if lamarckian inheritance were a fact, evolution would still be non-lamarckian."[25] Darwin, without excluding use and disuse as supplementary factors, considered natural selection as the main reason for the many apparently purposeful variations in animal and plant type and for the many new variations without purpose and plan remaining hereditary. Inanimate elements emerging automatically and without purpose or plan from an environment accessible to the organism by chance, he regarded as the origin of very minimal favorable hereditary variations. In the struggle for existence forced on organisms by overproduction, only those species best suited to the environment were preserved.

The opponents raised the objection that Darwin could not explain how a completely directionless variation could be reconciled with the obvious tendency of living protoplasm to respond to periodically recurring processes with advantageous modification and with the development of useful characteristics. Examples are the rapid renewal of blood after severe loss; regeneration of tissues after injuries; joining of partial functions to form complicated and more purposeful ones; the development of lower elements of form into higher ones and into organs assuring greater permanency of the individual and of the species. The end-result—they believe—is produced more by the advantages of a mere chance situation than by those of organisation.

The objection that adaptive results, for instance the human eye, the wing of the bird, the mimicry of the butterfly, are not to be explained by chance and automatic processes of mutation, was not the only one. Paleontologists observing fossils came to the conclusion that their trend had been not at all adaptive. The fossil animals evolved, not in one single direction toward a useful goal, but in a direction both useless and disadvantageous, even destructive. (Orthogenesis)

The geneticists, in their turn, advance the argument proved by Weismann, that it is impossible to convert modifications originating from environment into hereditary variations and that the adaptation as assumed by Darwin does not exist at all. Such variations were always replaced within a few generations by the original characteristics. The change in the modified organism arises by means of genetic factors and those changes which are always taking place in the chromosomes, the mutations, are in no way predominantly adaptive and, on the contrary, often very harmful. Natural selection usually leads to extinction i.e.: to the elimination of those unsuited for mutation. "What an organism is like is determined by its whole set of chromosomes. Adaptation seldom requires a single new mutation but an entire set coordinated in a new way." New characters and new types of plants and animals arise quite by chance and suddenly due to a change in the hereditary substance within the germ cell. The raw material of evolution is produced above all by mutation of the germ-cells to new forms. Each characteristic is produced by many genes. A single gene can participate in many characteristics. Characteristics, visible characters, change more often than the genes. As soon as a germ-variation has arisen, it influences the perpetuation of all the genetic factors which form the organism. Hereditary change does not occur by gradual change. The germ-plasm can change into a new species only suddenly. The conversion of genetically lower into genetically higher races is only possible by crossing—coupling or separation of hereditary Mendelian factors—or by sudden variation due to unknown causes.[26] The environment is not able to change those autonomous hereditary units which are always present in great numbers and which are indivisible and independent of one another. These are transferred from generation to generation and constitute the total hereditary endowment.

How little the unilateral theories of the paleontologists and geneticists as well as the theory of sudden mutation of De Vries, have been able to displace that of Darwin is evident from the fact that today his theory is considered "the most advanced scientific discipline in general biology, one, where calculation can predict results to be later verified by experiment and where pure theory can suggest profitable lines of advance."

According to G. G. Simpson[27] "the correct answer on natural selection is not *if* this is or is not the cause of adaptation, but *how* adaptation arises in the interplay of multiple forces of which Darwinian natural selection is obviously one of many."

Characters as such are not inherited whether they are

24

acquired or not. It is a series of determinants for a developmental system that is inherited. Which characters result from this depends on the interplay of the inherited determinants, the activities of the organism and the environment during development.

Recent investigations lead to the recognition that without selection long continued straight-line evolution towards higher specialization could not occur. Natural selection is not only not impossible, as many had believed, but without it new integrated organisms could not have arisen at all. Most mutations are small ones, the change resulting only gradually by progressive change during the course of generations. The mutations are often masked in their effect by environmental modifications. An uncommon small selective advantage can assure the preservation of favored genes and a more favorable hereditary gene combination.

Consideration of experiences made in the various branches of investigation demonstrated the necessity for the formulation of a synthetic theory. Natural selection is today a valid essential factor of evolution, just as Darwin assumed. However, a factor overlooked until now has attained great significance: *Pre-adaptation.*

"The smaller and simpler the living units considered the greater the probability that the atomic and molecular units composing them might come together by mere chance." [28] "The structural and physiological peculiarities arising at random may prove to be suitable or useful in the environment of the organism or any other environment available to it." [29]

In short, pre-adaptations, acting more slowly and more cumulatively than the large and small adaptations, a large mass of repeated germ changes of reciprocal genetic adaptations and perhaps also other factors not controlled by chance but selectively joined to produce the final result. They created quite mechanically, without the plan of a causal agent, a relatively sudden radical change in the habits, environment and structure. They thus formed the conditions for a new and advantageous use of the means at hand. Even in an essentially constant environment, changes in structure can give rise to changes in orientation and to germ changes and variations, and thus become an integrating part of the continuation of life.

All new animal and plant types which by chance deviate from the normal have found a pathway adapted to their peculiarity. This somehow strikes us like Lamarck's old idea in reverse.

Obviously, because of the many changes which the evolution theory had to undergo, Lamarck's theory still has a few supporters today, not counting the work of Lysenko, since this is unscientific and was set up only to support a social theory. Indeed, Lamarckism may be of subordinate importance for evolution today. However, the assumption that the effect of environment and of use and disuse on the genes is no more than zero, should not be hastily made. One can never be certain whether the prevailing theory of today may not also be merely an approach to the truth.

The need for replacing the many previous theories by a synthetic theory, and the experience that the law of energy has been proved valid, though only a short while ago, nobody expected it to be,[30] suggests that environmental forces are among the innumerable factors participating in the development bringing about species-adaptations as well as failures.

The working hypothesis that the law of energy is valid without exception explains the puzzle of how during millions of years by means of concerted action of separate lifeless elements arising without any purpose or goal, pre-adaptations could have arisen and how finally life was adapted to the environment.

Chapter II

a) The motive for self-preservation of the unicellular being and the progressive organization of the multi-cellular. Centers of regulation of vegetative and animal functions, of affectivity and of the highest mental performances.

b) Manifestations of inner excitation:—associated movements, imitation, etc. together form a primitive language.

c) Brain and mind. The relations between single sections of the brain and talent-variants.

d) Evolution and articulated speech. Changes in Organs accompanying articulated speech. Pathological disturbances of articulated speech.

e) Speech and Thought. Peculiarities of the primitive mind. Dominance of isolated observations. Picture representations. Preconceptions. Superstitions. Absence of abstract concepts. Just as striving toward a goal is not a general characteristic of nature, reasonable purposeful behavior is not a human characteristic. Just as old habits originally protective, if fixed too long, can endanger life, so holding to old prejudices can also threaten the existence of man.

f) Nowhere does nature advance by leaps. This is shown by the history of art and science as well as by all reforms and revolutions. No wonder that the average man learns so slowly to select from the vast quantity of phantasy-combinations those which are reasonable.

To get an illustration of how life arose, we need but look at an amoeba wandering on a border between light and dark with perfect regularity. The amoeba turns toward the light.[31] The drive for selfpreservation, a characteristic by which all living beings differ from dead masses, compels it to behave this way. Light is indispensable to it for the assimilation of food.

Less evident than the fact that for preserving life in the living protoplasm the substance unceasingly taken away by the outside has to be restored, is the answer to the question: what induces it to preserve itself, to multiply and so on?

Supposing that, though the impression by a single stimulus is imperceptible, the colloidal mass of the living cell gets finally hypersensitive if submitted to the action of a series of stimuli, we get a better understanding of what really happens. We have reason to believe that frequent repetition of stimuli can give rise at the same time to a change in the structure of the protoplasm and to the emergence of a kind of monitor, i.e. a *trace* of perception that there exist some outside forces different from the Ego.

The hypothesis that lifeless matter could have been so changed by the action of a multitude of irritations set in motion, that the whole variety of functions and organs characteristic to living beings developed, is in full harmony with experience.

That the number of irritations brought into play might have been enormous is suggested by the calculation

28

that the number of excitations must increase geometrically if sensation is to be increased arithmetically[32]

The needs of the unicellular organism are so primitive —its metabolism is assured by such simple processes as diffusion and osmosis—that every part can still substitute another, if this be incapable of functioning. Like a Robinson Crusoe confined to his island, such an organism can supply all its needs alone. The maintenance of its equilibrium seems not to differ much from inertia, the attribute of every inanimate mass, visible as resistance against change. Both are easily understood, as it were, as internal movements produced by outside forces. In short, the way of how living organism reacts with internal movements upon those of external forces differs from the inertia of the lifeless matter (its resistance against change) only in that, the sensitiveness acquired after previous irritations serves as struggle toward self-preservation. This is an aim taken over by the parts into which the propagating and reproducing mothercell divides.

We have now to explain how the various functions of organs of multicellular organisms originated, and how on the one hand the progressive organisation, on the other improvement in the mutual balance of functions and organs were gradually achieved.

Obviously the maintenance of regular function of a multicellular organism with assured mutual adaptation of the large number of cells resulting from the division of the mothercell, required the development of many specific organs, suitable for the orderly functioning of the cell-state and the performance of most varied functions. These organs were needed for more than a purely mechanical attachment of the cell-beings put alongside each other.

To understand how the forces within the interior of a single member of the multicellular organism and those of its environment are acting on one another and are

29

mutually related, we need but compare it with a human settlement in the process of formation. As every member of a human settlement is faced with the solution of problems as, for instance, transportation, distribution etc., unknown to the individual living in isolation, so their unequal predisposition and position compels the individual members of a cell-community to try to satisfy its needs. The result is that, in time, there develops progressively a greater differentiation of activity, inclinations, habits and capacity.

Such a comparison renders the survey of the intertwined relationship of the cells easier.

Differentiation of performances parallels that of the organs. Function, however, probably became noticeable prior to the formation of the corresponding organ.

For the building up and the breaking down of substances, for their supply and removal and for their absorption and distribution there was required an entire system of organs, the vegetative system. Besides the organs of digestion, the urinary and sexual apparatus, the blood and lymph vessels developed. A necessary complement of the vegetative system was the large nervous system. This included the muscular, the peripheral and central system and the sensory apparatus which assured the connections between the organism and its environment.

These organ-systems are able to produce muscular contraction and glandular secretion. However, their existence in no way explains the organic interaction taking place synchronously or at intervals in the different organs.

For example, it does not explain how a far distant hormone, necessary for the function of an organ, is produced at exactly the required moment; how after an injury to the tissues of an organism there immediately develop physico-chemical energies producing regeneration; how the organism reduces its secretion of fluids to a minimum when in danger of desiccation and by inducing a feeling of thirst takes care of the rapid replacement of fluids; nor how, as in the case of feeling of thirst, there emerge at other times warnings such as hunger, fatigue, urge for sleep, chills, pain, malaise, discomfort and sickness.[33]

The proved correlation between the performances of the various parts of the organism requires the assumption of a center in which all the fibers converge and which regulate the behavior of the entire organism. Although each individual cell has the capacity for action, other arrangements are necessary for the regulation of activity in an organ, so that if a muscle receives an impulse to contract, its antagonist receives an impulse to release some of its tension, in other words: "throwing one reflex into action inhibits another."

Analogous to the phenomenon of motion, nervous activity and inhibition manifest themselves by secretory and sensory phenomena. A special type of machinery is necessary to avoid conflicts in activity. Without its development rapid adaptation (emotional, psychic, voluntary) to normal and abnormal activity of the organs would be impossible. Feelings and sensations which reach the organism as signals of external or internal conditions, are switched and conducted further into the peripheral organs of execution such as the muscles, glands and sensory organs. These then react by contraction, secretion, perception and so forth.

It is known today that such a center does exist in the ganglia of the diencephalon for feelings, moods, affects and reflexes connected with them. In a word, they are responsible for total affectivity.

In animals with a narrow brain covering, stimulation, depending on the place stimulated, can result in inhibition, excitation, sleep or a maniacal attack.

The cerebrum is not necessary for such performances. This can be observed experimentally in a frog in which the entire cerebrum has been removed. Tickling it with a straw can set it into anxiety and rage.

31

Affective mimicry is an interbestial language. The suckling reacts with complete understanding to affective expressions such as caressing sounds and disapproving tones. Desire and listlessness, strong emotional tone toward sexual objects are older than the cerebral cortex and affectivity is not lost in the most severe brain diseases.

Recollection of individual experiences is a preliminary condition for the development of phantasy and reason.

A special center exists in the cerebral cortex and thalamus for the highest function of the human mind. "In it the demand from the periphery is supplied by the cerebral cortex." [34]

Friedrich Kraus differentiates between two kinds of systems: the cortical person, or one in whom the cerebral cortex predominates; and the inferior person (*Tiefenperson*) regulating the visceral apparatus, i.e.: the heart activity, metabolism and breathing as well as the sensory apparatus of impulses.

More detailed discussion is necessary to explain how man was able to develop such complicated performances as those of his intellect. Experience again and again shows that it is inward excitation which sets a human being into motion.

Drive and activity are the expressions of the inner irritation already to be observed in the newborn. The greater the tension the greater the desire for release, discharge. The type, direction, strength and duration of the excitation, the effects of drives combined with those of environmental forces determine the kind of human needs. To satisfy a dominating urge, both the moving force of an inner irritation and a favorable environment are necessary.

The assumption that every externally perceptible action of the organism corresponds to a state of inner excitation seems physiologically well founded. It can be demonstrated that concentration on an object increases the amount of blood whose supply is needed to release the energies claimed by the increased engagement of the particular parts of the brain participating in the action. Even with very slight excitation the blood flows toward the head of the prone person.

The influence of positive affects as, for instance, joy, in the sense of dilatation of the cerebral blood vessels is experimentally demonstrable.[35] There could be established in the parts of the brain affected at the same time a rise in temperature and changes in the excretion of phosphates, the ion concentration and the local electrical action current. Changes of pulse corresponding to excitation have been observed.

The effective components of our sensations, perceptions and images corresponding to the inner tension, decide how we react: with a movement, with a readiness to look directly at an object, to clear an indistinct image etc. According to its type an affect may carve a path for a perception or make the path difficult or even isolate the perception, by switching the power of passions. The emotional tone of an object can be so intense that it compels preoccupation with it and represses all other thoughts. What is not of interest does not disturb the mental equilibrium and is forgotten as immaterial. Affect can induce us to make a perception, to pay attention to it, to brood over it, but also, on thinking it over, not include it in our calculation.

Throughout history we can follow up the role that passion played in human accomplishments which would have been forever out of reach on the basis of mere reasonable reflection. The saying of Lassalle: "without suffering not a single stone is separated from another in history," is confirmed by experience. Emotion can likewise lift us up to the highest tension as well as paralyze the power of our spirit and of our body. For instance, a sudden danger proved capable of delivering the occupants of a ship from seasickness.

Externally emotion becomes noticeable by the move-

33

ments accompanying it. Among those which are coordinated toward a definitive purpose may be mentioned: gestures and concomitant movements of the body in laughing, crying, howling, yelling, speaking. dancing, pantomime, and so forth. A threat is made with the hand as if to strike a blow; the fist is balled as if to attack an enemy, one bites in anger, sticks out his tongue in hate and caresses in love. We tremble with anxiety, shout with joy, vomit with disgust. Here too belong the kissing and licking of animals, as when tasting perhaps something sweet, signifying merely the sucking reflex at the mother's breast. Embracing as a symbol of affection is simple reproduction of the embrace in mating. Excitation is further expressed by the mimicking movements of pantomime and by the symbolic movements of the band masters. By raising and lowering his arm or whole body he shows whether high or low tones are to be played as well as the tempo by the speed of his movements.[36]

These movements are especially significant in that they repeat the excitation of which they are the expression distinctly enough to render it also understandable to other individuals. The same holds true of people from different regions who had never had contact with one another. Thus the same affect is accompanied by the same movements. Even animals and man understand each other, though to a limited degree.

These symbols thus become a means of understanding, a primitive language.

Merely the movement of a person nearby reveals the affect which lay at the basis of his movement: a painful expression of the face which we perceive conveys to us, simultaneously with the expression of pain, also the pain itself. In the same way sadness, joy, boredom, fatigue, despair, apathy and sympathy are conveyed, even if the person does not realize it.

Attentive observation of the environment is vital for

those who are to understand it. If the child is to have its needs satisfied, not only does the mother have to understand the child, but likewise the child to understand the mother. Ignorance of what a person really needs renders effective assistance impossible.

By instinctive repetition and imitation of the movements of other persons, we convey affections. Gesticulations, cries etc. become a medium of understanding. Just as the instinct by stimulating imitation constitutes the bridge from the unconscious to the conscious, so the reflex [37] is the transition between the physical and the unconscious. With frequent repetition of gestures and tones the fragments necessary for understanding are reduced, occasionally even, to just a single word.

How vital it is for the individual to look around for models and to imitate members of the species, so as not to run the danger of having his drives lead him to purposeless or entirely inappropriate actions, is evident from the extraordinary extensive imitation in the animal world. In amphibians, birds and many mammals there is a strong impulse to produce instinctive cries. Thorndike doubts that animals can learn to do things by mere imitation after having seen others doing them. "They don't transform any incidental response into a deep-rooted habit." [38] "Dogs do not learn any new tricks purely by imitation. . . . Some birds are strongly influenced by the songs they hear while growing up." The first sounds of birds in captivity were not dependent on imitation. However, the song became peculiar to themselves and quite different from that of the free bird. As they became older they assumed the song of the birds in the same area. Their neighbors served more as models than their parents. "The lamb follows his mother and has, by the time it is weaned, formed strong habits of gregariousness which persist throughout life. But bottle-fed lambs do not respond to calls of their fellows and in the pasture they graze in solitude, paying little attention to the rest of the group. But the basic tendency to form associations is not lost; they learn to follow human beings much as a normal sheep follows his proper kin."

The same is observed in birds. They follow the mother and are rewarded with a worm. The imitation of apes has become proverbial. "The individual ape is an individual but no personality, a strongly entrenched member of his band. Ceremony, play, sleep and activity from the leader ape to the last member of the band is orderly and strictly regulated."[39] While they imitate they follow a drive with renunciation of every trace of their own mental activity.

That man too is primarily a creature of drive is shown by the extent of imitation, not only in children and in savages. "Men as well as women lose their individuality in certain social situations leading to mass-hysterias, lynchings, contagious emotions which rob individuals of personal initiative and independent thought." Laughing, yawning and coughing are known to be infectious. Mass effects of the avalanche-like spread of emotions include: castefeeling; war psychoses; epidemics of insanity.

Imitation has a great deal to do with the origin of customs, usages and modes. At the time of Charles II of England studies in physical laboratories were the great vogue; during Molière's time, in France, theatre shows; at the court of Frederick I. of Prussia, frugality. The successs of the anatomical school of Vesalius in Padua started a series of similar schools in other cities. The fashion to treat all possible diseases with leeches resulted in the application of 100,000 leeches during a single year (1819) in the hospital of a small place.

Imitation plays a great part also in the arts. This is not only because of the great amount of copying of already existing works. In the lowest form, art is imitation of nature. "Dur-scala: imitation of tones in the horizontal, in succession; accords: imitation in the vertical, conjointly." (Schönberg.)

36

Often imitation of gestures and movements, those primeval symbols, is of inestimable value. This medium by which primitive language acts, is often indispensable for influencing large masses of individuals, since in such cases the power of logical conviction fails.

The comparatively late development of articulate speech explains why it often lags in efficiency behind the primitive sign language. Tendency toward a sign language is already observed in dogs, cats and even in frogs. In the anthropoid apes it is said to be highly developed, as Garner has claimed, having observed by sound plates. Gorillas and chimpanzees each possess their own peculiar idiom, incomprehensible to the other species. This view, however, has not been confirmed by more recent investigations. On the contrary: "There is not a single authentic record of spontaneous imitation of human speech by any of the other primates, even though chimpanzees and gorillas have spent years in close association with men. The best ape students have mastered no more than one or two very simple words and in no instance has there been any proof that the meaning of the words was understood. The real reason: the absence of a degree of mental development high enough to support the complex of intellectual activities essential to true language."

Tamed animals do not learn by watching human beings to perform acts completely foreign to their natural repertoire of behavior. Julius, the orangutang of Prof. R. M. Yerkes[40] never learned to open a padlock with a key though he was shown many times. He failed to learn by instruction how to handle the tool.

The behavior of the ape like that of other animals, is still fixed within narrow limits. The social mechanism still plays a subordinate role in comparison to the biological one. The conditions are still lacking under which a human culture could develop. The anatomical structure of the ape brain, the predominance of the cerebral lobes and the great extension of the visual cortex marks him as a purely "visual animal."

A gradual quantitative extension of the association-areas of the brain was required for the development of a more plastic brain-mechanism and of the capacity for greater rationality in the selection of ideas that are fit for mental performance of greater biological importance. Cerebral function cannot improve until new paths are carved, i.e.: until the anatomical structure is changed. Such changes as organ-growth, improved efficiency and progress mature slowly. The various areas of the cerebral cortex do not mature at the same time. The intelligence as well as the cerebral cortex of the child mature in stages. The gradual maturation of mental capacities is also indicated by the variations in the structure of the brain convolutions, to be found according to the type of talent.

Comparison of brain-casts seems to indicate that the development of intelligence and of the brain go hand in hand.

The weight of the brain of an adult gorilla is about 580 grams, no more than that of a newborn child.[41] That of an Australian aborigine is no more than that of a 9 year old European. The weight of the adult European's brain is 1500 grams; in extremely brilliant personalities it has been found much greater. Turgeniev's and Helmholtz's brains each weighed 2000 gr. The weight of Cuvier's was so great that the scale was checked for accuracy.

The size of the brain and brain-case, however, is not the only determining factor for the degree of intelligence, capacity of judgment, memory and combination of talent. Some mentally deficient individuals have large brains. The largest has been found to belong to an imbecile. There are artists with small brains. Voltaire's brain-case was small. However, when it was opened, the mass and circumference of the brain-substance aroused astonishment. The brain of Anatole France was lighter than average in weight, those of Gauss, the mathematician, G. Stanley Hall, psychologist, and of William Osler, surgeon, showed no essential differences in weight from the weight of the brain of the average person.[42]

The fact that the brain of man exceeds that of animals in mass is explained by the addition of a series of new brain-parts. These are bearers of newly acquired functions which are absent in lower animals and which are considered the basis for becoming human.[43]

As compared with the primitive brain of lower animals, the crown and frontal sinus region of the brain of the diluvian man have become wider and higher. The indispensable association apparatus for the highest mental functions, constituting only a small fragment of the brain mass in the primitive brain, has developed into the main mass in the brain of the adult civilized man. The remaining portions of the brain, especially those connected with the sensory organs, have become reduced in mass.

Many consider the forebrain the seat of higher intellectual functions, of attention and of higher personality. The higher receptive capacities are connected with the integrity of the parietal lobes. An essential part in the origin of mental capacities is ascribed by others to the endocrine glands, such as the hypothalamic (posterior hypophyseal adrenal), the medullary complex, that is the pituitary body at the base of the brain, the adrenals etc.

Anatomical findings indicate that the number of formed path-ways as well as the liberation of paths to the cerebral cortex, are perhaps more important for the capacity of performance of the brain than the size,[44] and that certain variants in the development of individual sections of the brain correspond to certain talents.[45] In the famous lecturer, Gambetta, autopsy showed an unusually great development of the speech center, (Broca's frontal convolution); in an especially talented designer a special variant in the region of the calcarina. In the painter, Adolf Menzel, a left-handed person, an asymmetry of the brain surface in favor of the right hemisphere was present. The third brain convolution predominated, the course of the furrow on the left being throughout simpler and clearer. The convolutions on the right showed more segmentation, increased surfaces and convolutions. There were formations in places on the right which were absent on the left. There was above all an increase in the substance of the central nervous tissue at the fronto-occipital and temporal brain. It is uncertain whether this was due to a congenital variant of talents or to the effect of permanent unilateral use.[46] V. Economo[47] considers this to be functionally acquired. He sees proof of the special optical designing endowment in the considerable surface enlargement of the right occipital lobe.

Since the brain-findings do not too clearly explain the difference between great intellectual performance and the poor performance of the moron, the recently found striking differences in the caliber of blood vessels supplying the nutrition of the brain and brain coverings were estimated as related to the differences in performances. Reports in the daily newspapers[48] recently advanced the view that a team of neuro-surgeons in cooperation with other specialists may succeed "by adding new vessels to the ones of restricted caliber in the brain coverings to foster the intellectual capacity of the average man to higher levels."[49] Unfortunately, hope of increasing mental capacity in this way has no more foundation than the use of glutonic acid, the efficacy of which was not confirmed by recent investigations.

Physiologists and pathologists point out that their experiences with the great increase in the formation of blood vessels and their regression during and after pregnancy respectively, sufficiently indicate that the greater caliber of the vessels of the brain coverings are

40

the result of greater functional participation of the brain rather than of "superior mental endowment."

To grasp the transformation into the human species we must consider, in addition to the development of the brain, also the development of articulate speech.

Such primitive signs as cries, gestures, behaviorisms, noises, only make man succeed in conveying to his associates his own inner excitation, to warn them of danger. But they do not convey easily and unequivocally the finer shades of man's more complicated experiences to his companions or to later generations.

At first, the primitive man, when flying into a passion, freed by his upright position, had to support his gestures and noises by the accompanying movements of his arms. In order to free his arm his forefoot had to be transformed into a hand and the animal which had climbed down from the tree had to learn to walk upright. This in itself required an advanced development of the brain.

Once freed by the upright bearing, hands and arms became fit to be used for grasping and for breaking food into smaller parts. In correlation with this the whole face changed. Teeth receded; changes appeared in the teeth, the chewing musculature, lips, tongue, palate, throat, larynx. Similarly, changes occured in the voice and in the resonance apparatus, ever better adapted to one another, and also in breathing. Thus the necessary conditions for the expression of vowels, consonants, syllables and words were created. The cerebral cortex made up abundantly for the stunted sense of smell of the now walking nomad searching the world for food.

The combination of the numerous mental impressions due to the upright position with the play instinct gradually led to the development of phantasy and understanding. These in turn created the conditions necessary for the development of an organ entirely independent of the body: Human civilization.

The integrity of the speech muscles and of their nerve

41

supply, together with the drive for companionship made language an instrument of communication; however, they were insufficient to make it also an instrument of reasoning.

For the transmission of thoughts from one person to another, clear language is not enough. The words have to be retained and their meaning understood by speaker and listener, through common experiences.

The normal child does not develop these partial capabilities at the same time. It learns to repeat the word earlier than to comprehend its sense; earlier to copy the picture of a letter than to understand its meaning. To compound into one general concept facts belonging to the same class is what the human being learns last.

Just like the partial capacities required for normal speech, reading and thinking arose independently, so they might be lost again in the same way, i.e., by brain lesions. A well known object might be recognized, but the word corresponding to it no longer written; the picture of a letter in a picture book still recognized, but the letter no more read; the word-sense no longer stated, the single sound no more combined to form the whole intelligible picture. The destruction of the cortical motor center in the sulcus Rolandi is followed by the annihilation of personal and pantomimic movements and gestures. After the destruction of the connections between visual center and hearing, the understanding of speech remains and spontaneous speech and repetition is retained, but the ability to read and write are disturbed. When the connections between hearing-speech center and Broca's center are disturbed, then the reflex speech and repetition of words is lost.

The different forms of speech-disturbances are known as word-deafness, word-blindness, mind-blindness and as aphasic-apraxic, sensory and amnesic aphasia.

Normal speech has tremendous significance for thought, since the spoken, written and printed word is

42

put into circulation and can even be passed on to later generations. Later generations are usually inclined to repeat what they have heard, and satisfied with pure imitation, which is easier than forming their own ideas. They are in the habit of using the old vocabulary as a means of understanding and will form new words only if the old ones prove to be inadequate.

The origin of new words varies greatly. The transformations may be brought about now by fusion of word fragments and meaningless syllables, now by the similarity of the sound, at another time even by the inability of the speaker to pronounce a word correctly. How a word came to be used as a symbol for reality, can often no longer be established. The legend of the Phoenix bird arose out of confusion between two similar hieroglyphics, one indicating "one century" and the other "bird." The legend created from this is an Arabic bird which was said to arise every 500 years and then to live for another 500 years.

However, it takes not always a long time before the meaning of a word becomes vague. The meaning of many words was already obscure when they were shaped. Primitive man was not able to coin words indicating something definite because he lacked the necessary mental schooling for clear concepts. The natives of British Guiana use words like "immun" or "keber" (the latter meaning, perhaps, food of the dead) sometimes to designate individual characteristics, sometimes the sum of characteristics, i.e., of things. The Melanesian does not perceive a definite number of things but a heap, a crowd, a group. The single individual, in his eyes, is only a part of a group to which he belongs, he is not a unit, but like a hand or a foot—a member. Since these ignorant and unlearned savages are guided only by sensory percepts and mystical feelings, they do not distinguish between the living and the nonliving. They become confused by the purely superficial similarity of things and confuse the real thing with its shadow, mirror-image, name, picture. Their easily fatigued minds simply take over what has been handed down from their forebears without any trace of a thirst for knowledge, with no judgment, just as in play. They do not distinguish between subject and object, phantasy and reality. They consider a single organ, a single function as an independent being and find no contradiction in the idea that they themselves are the bird which they see flying in the air. If they are frightened or have their hopes aroused by natural phenomena which they cannot correctly interpret, they get into a state of excitation. The internal image based on these excitations, such as dreams, hallucinations, arouse in them the belief that they are surrounded by mystical powers which they seek to influence by exorcism.[50]

Unable to separate that which he has seen from that which he has thought, primitive man is inclined to believe whatever he feels and vice versa, to feel whatever he believes and in his thinking is limited purely to preconcepts, prenotions. Experiences such as the following, reported by Karl von Steinen, show why he cannot grasp clear concepts. "The Bakiri are suffocated by the abundance of their supply and cannot manage it economically. They trade only in small coins and are to be called rich rather than poor in the number of pieces. The general concept "palm tree" is completely lacking; they absorb isolated bits of knowledge without bothering about general concepts. Every parrot has its own name."

The clarity necessary for the formation of general concepts did not permeate man until very late. Primitive man can only grasp images. His dreams are images: "symbolic representations of occurrences in unusual disguise."[51] His speech is also symbolic, his oldest writing is picture writing, hieroglyphics. He loves symbols and similes. The first literary productions are myths, legends, fables, fairy tales, parables. The emotional emphasis of

44

perceptions prevents man from viewing his environment objectively. Thus his first evaluations become prejudices.

That this primitive stage of thinking observable in savages is still far from being overcome is shown by the large diffusion of superstition. How far the superstition had been extended even among the cultured peoples of antiquity, is evident from the fact that even the most learned Greeks and Romans participated in the calling of spirits.[52] A protocol engraved in a stone, discoverered in Cos, the native city of Hippocrates, reads as related by Mommsen: "In the temple of Cos one laid himself down and awaited dreams revealing the method of healing and the departure of the disease."

Man did not acquire the ability to form abstract concepts until late. The writings of the Babylonians and Assyrians contain descriptions of single processes, concrete things, individual symptoms of disease, isolated observations, snapshots. The old Greek writings contain at times accurate descriptions of entire symptom-complexes of diseases well known today, such as mumps and diphtheria, but any sort of definition is lacking. The diseases are not even named.

The formation of abstract concepts did only begin at the time of Plato.

The preliminary condition for finer differentiations was conceptual thinking: formation of a thought thing by abstracting from concrete things a series of common characteristics and by their designation with a suitable word. By adding supplementary words like "recurrens," "intermittens" etc. to the word "febris," which embraced a whole group of symptoms named "fever," memory was relieved, since the addition of "intermittens" to the word fever, signified the specific influence of quinine upon this kind of fever.

Any blank or interruption within a series of similar things or things considered to belong to one another, which points to the existence of some difference, creates the urge of selecting two different terms in place of a single one, thus, for "living being" two terms "plant" and "animal" were shaped in order not to let fall into oblivion the newly acquired knowledge.

As knowledge increased, a new language arose. Each word formed a rung on the ladder which led upward in the understanding of nature. However, even the richest word building by itself would not have been sufficient if not supplemented by formation of sentences condensed to judgment.

In order to avoid misunderstanding in the evaluation of experiences, words had to be brought into a logical relation to one another, instead of being placed in any arbitrary position. Nouns, adjectives, conjunctions, verbs had to be placed in the correct position, had to be in the right order. The sentence, not the word is the psychological unit, the basis of all reasonable judgment. Reason decides when we have to say "the hare sees the lion," and when "the lion sees the hare."

The content of consciousness is not revealed in a manner fixed previously but while we are speaking. Not until he formed thought things, i.e. conceptions by abstraction has man become capable of forming sentences, i.e. judgments.

To aid him in the accomplishment of his vital aim, i.e. self-preservation, in a hostile environment, and in giving him dominance over it, man's judgment had to be based upon experience excluding error, i.e. based on reason and knowledge. He had to develop a more efficient instrument for the formation of the body: the human soul.

The fact, that inertia, i.e. perseverance, is a general characteristic alike of the lifeless and the living world, explains the difficulties man met when trying to satisfy his—at times—most urgent need.

Everywhere in the animal world we meet the inclination to hold fast to old habits long after the environment has changed essentially and they have become meaningless for the preservation of the species. We see many animals repeating their usual reflex-movements even when these have already become a danger to them.

Adaptation to a new situation often takes many generations. One explanation for the origin of the gigantic size of many inhabitants of the prehistoric world, the mammoths, saurians etc., is that the unlimited continuation of their habitual greed for food made their weight increase so much that they became helpless and died in the marshes. The formless antlers which once served the giant stag as protection and defense became merely a handicap as they became overgrown.[53]

There are of course, attempts to explain this phenomenon of gigantism, as due to progressive pituitary development with loss of capacity for reproduction.[54] Furthermore, the assumption of many paleontologists, that these animals may have become overwhelmed by the ice age and died in great numbers seems plausible, since at certain spots masses of bone-collections of these animals have been found.

Even if we renounce using the first named explanation as proof against the assumption of the struggle toward a goal as general characteristic of living nature, science procures yet other proofs showing that the struggle is often not only not purposeful, but purposeless, quite inappropriate, even contradictory.[55] As proof may suffice to cite the occurrence of congenital malformations. Also, to recall that pain, the original purpose of which was to inform the center of a danger threatening at the periphery in order to induce a purposeful reaction, causes the rheumatic patient to put his muscles to rest, whilst he would be better off by getting them in motion. Or else to remember that pain in neuralgia, tabes, cancer, becomes man's enemy due to its excessiveness. . . . In a word: what was originally intended to preserve, leads man to his destruction. Fever, inflammation, coagulation

47

of blood, although originally serving to preserve the organism, can become a danger to it e.g. coagulated blood, instead of stopping a hemorrhage, can become a fatal embolus.

The same earth worms which by loosening the earth facilitated the task of the ploughing farmer may cause damage by spreading infection. It is not the purpose of a gall-producing plant to assure, by feeding a parasite, the maintenance of its existence any more than it is the purpose of a smoker to procure for the beggar the enjoyment of smoking by throwing away a cigar stump. Smoker and beggar, plant and parasite pursue their own purpose. It is not the struggle toward a goal, but plant, animal and man act whenever some longing, some urge, demands satisfaction.

All occurrences we observe, are products of the interplay of elements of a force called Nature. Its components associate, dissociate, combine, dissolve in the most varied ways. It is man himself who, being concerned with his own preservation evaluates every happening according to the degree it serves or does not serve or even hampers his purposes. However, all living beings including man, set up goals for themselves as often as some need induces them to do so, though—to be sure—they often fail in satisfying their needs.

Of special interest among those processes of nature which we are used to summarize as "life," are on the one hand the origin of the tendency of living protoplasm to maintain itself, on the other hand that of its peculiar plasticity, i.e. its capacity to be modeled. There are, for instance, insects capable of perceiving ultraviolet rays inaccessible to our senses and aquatic animals sensing the pressure of the streaming current.

Is it not amazing that, in spite of the endowment of many animals with better senses than those of man, he surpasses all the other animals as far as the highest intellectual capacities are concerned? In lower animals, the

48

shorter life span and the limited space for the development of their nerve centers is the simple explanation.

However, what are the facts in the case of higher animals? To them higher mental performance is not as inaccessible as has been believed previously. They are capable of observing and recalling concrete experiences. They possess even a language; to be sure, one limited to gestures and noises. By training they even can get induced to solve tasks which are entirely new to the individual, i.e. they are capable of mental performances not inherited by particular species. For instance: mice and rats learn in time to avoid errors they had made at the beginning and reach the goal in a much shorter way. In a puzzle cage, labyrinth or maze, they even learn to open several locks.[56] . . . All of Wolfgang Köhler's apes easily learned to use a stick to get an object beyond their reach. After having succeeded in using the stick spontaneously and correctly the first time—this happened always suddenly without previous rehearsing—they seized the next time a more or less suitable object, i.e. a stick or a blade of a straw. They thus proved that they understood how to insert a bridge between their aim and themselves, that they knew how the stick would function.

That the animal does not need to imitate old movements for getting to the essential kernel of the performance is a sign of intelligence.

That chimpanzees own the capacity to abstract the idea of color from the different shapes of two-colored objects, that is, to consider the color alone, has been demonstrated by Nadie Kohts.[57] And that chimpanzees are capable of forming concepts and getting insight in the meaning of the connection of events, has been observed by Yerkes. These experiences suggest that the gap between animal and man can be bridged, in other words: that the difference is but one of degree, not of kind. The language of many savages also is rudimentary, so is, too, their level of civilization.

The amount of experience and time needed to bring the savage, roaming the world in search of food, to the point to become transmuted into what we call "civilized man," we can only guess. There is reason to believe that bad experiences more than happy occurrences have contributed to the unfolding of his mind. However, in time he overcame the obstacles and was able to develop his mind to the point that it gave rise to myths, religion, justice, morality, skill and knowledge.

To get an explanation of what really happened we do well to recall that peeping at something is, as it were, an extension of touching.[58] In similar way we can consider imagination as an extension of seeing. There is only a difference in the degree of excitation, no sharp boundary between those phantasms which appear without former sensory perceptions and those stimulated by them.

Doubtless, before man had progressed enough not to feel satisfied with combinations which were rather the products of an inflamed fancy than based on experience, he first had to arrange during a very long time numberless observations succeeding one another. To realize that reasonable action is conditioned by the ability of establishing firmly in memory the most important experiences and fitting them to each other, man had to be aided by traditional language and ideas. Searching and testing by trial and error, though at first unconsciously, later more by conscious learning, he found by degrees the path leading him upwards to the development of science, knowledge, technical perfection.

The entire history of humanity, of the individual personality striving toward great mental height as well as that of the very slowly following masses, confirms the old saying that nature does not advance in leaps. Every successful attempt at fundamental change has been preceded by lesser unsuccessful ones.

The subjection of Egypt and Asia accomplished by

Alexander the Great, had been already planned before by Cimon the Athenian. The great seafarers of the Renaissance only repeated what the Normans had attempted before them. "The frightful catastrophe which completely overturned Europe and swallowed the Hapsburg Monarchy," writes Rudolf Sieghart in discussing the events between 1848 and 1918, "left the populations with their old cares and affected the inner nature of things very little. In spite of all attempts of finding a solution, from radical absolutism to radical democracy, conquest and compromise has been attempted; and, although all problems of the monarchy had been exposed, not one single problem has been solved."

Edouard Herriot writes in "Wellspring and Liberty":[59] "The complete suppression of all interior custom duties and customs in the whole realm of revolutionized France of 1789 was not a sudden one. The French revolution had been preceded by a long evolution in the direction of liberty, the tendency of which had been to fuse the parts into a great whole. . . . The same tendency for unification over as large an area as possible as in this "Europe en miniature," as France has also been called, is found in the United States, in England, in Central Europe and today, in the demand for "One World."

The same slowness of development is characteristic of all the different manifestations of the human mind. Its conscious state is preformed in the unconscious. Its change always proceeds gradually. Feelings, passions, sympathies, antipathies develop but slowly, even after having been recognized as based on prejudices. To kindle great passions—this concerns the individual as well as entire populations—requires always much time, therefore they always have a long preliminary history. The momentary flaring up of the love of a Romeo and Juliet, or a hate such as destroyed the Atrids in five generations, is always prepared by earlier generations. "A god does not immediately produce the idol or the monster. A

51

succession of noble and evil people finally bring joy or horror into the world."[60]

Bursts of anger resulting explosively in revolutions, are always preceded by numerous pin pricks. The burning violence which characterized the hate between Christians and Heretics in Spain during the Middle Ages, required centuries of prolonged fighting during many generations before it reached its summit.

Convictions, dogmas, conscious will, thinking, normal as well as pathological states of mind develop in the same way. Mental disease, as can often be demonstrated clearly, is frequently preceded by an observable premorbid state.

One people takes over from another the external elements of a religious creed only, not the inner feeling. An author notes: "That which in history is known as the Christian Movement had been alive previously for centuries in religions and sects." A superstition such as that Friday is a day of misfortune, even if long recognized to be an error, can prevent a person from undertaking something of importance on that day.

The same slow change occured in speech,[61] writing, vocations, art appreciation, scientific judgment, technique and method. To create the word-symbols "Monad" and "Prestabilized Harmony," two concepts imagined by Leibnitz, took this philosopher no less than five and ten years respectively.

Like speech, writing developed extremely slowly. It began with the depiction of definitive objects, animals, people, flowers and later developed to the stage of the stone covered with figures, symbols. It aimed at first at the designation of names and then gradually also at that of thoughts, feelings and actions. The first alphabet unintentionally arose from the most frequent designations for sounds of single syllables, single vowels, or in the course of time, for such in combination with consonants.

At the time of Osiris I., in ancient Egypt, there existed

characters for words, objects, syllables and also for the individual letters. The word "Osiris" was expressed by two hieroglyphic characters, one for the syllable "Os" and the second for "ris." One vowel and two consonants were used for "Ammon."[62]

According to Rappoport,[63] the Egyptians had made the wonderful analysis of sounds without which the invention of an alphabet would be impossible. They had set aside certain of their hieroglyphic symbols and given them alphabetical significance. They had learned to write their words with the help of this alphabet. It seems as if, in the course of a few generations, they must have come to see how unnecessary was the cruder form of picture writing which this alphabet would naturally supplant; but, in point of fact, they never did come to a realization of this seemingly simple proposition. Generation after generation and century after century they continued to use their same cumbersome complex writing and it remained for an outside nation to prove that the alphabet pure and simple was capable of fulfilling all the conditions of a written language."

As long as the art of writing remained rudimentary, its use was limited to the priest caste. The gradual improvement of the alphabet corresponding to the growing need for it, likewise the substitution of papyrus and parchment for stone and of the quill and later reed pen for the chisel (taking place with the cooperation of the Greeks) spread the art of writing. The substitution of connected writing—running hand—for distinctive letters, as well as the writing from left to right, used today in all European countries, came later still.

As slow as the development of language and writing was also that of other inventions. This is true not only of agriculturean art carried on unchanged in the same primitive way through ages—but likewise of the potter's work, the technique of which remained unchanged through centuries, as proved by excavations. Also, ship-

53

construction is with some savage races in a primitive state: a skiff built out of the hollow bark of a tree is still the "dernier cri." Steamship travel between Europe and the United States seemed unthinkable to many, hardly hundred years ago, because they believed that it was impossible to take along food and to build fueling stations along the way.

The same slowness in development can also be proved in science and legislation. Without having taken a firm hold with one's foot on the lower rung of the ladder one can not get onward even a single step. The time for carrying out great legislative reforms is not ripe the moment the scientific inquirer gets the conviction of its necessity, but only when the people themselves feel that they cannot do without them. To transfer feelings, convictions and thoughts, shared by the masses is much easier than to explain to them ideas differing considerably from theirs.

That it takes a long time for the masses to take notice of great new ideas has been often lamented by scientists. "The greatest thoughts are grasped last. . . . the light of the most distant star reaches man last and before it has arrived every person denies that there is such a star . . . how many centuries does a mind need for grasping concepts!"[64]

In a similar mood were written the following lines of two other great thinkers. "The most recent experiences," writes Goethe, after the failure of his publication "Die Horen," "have convinced me anew that instead of any true theoretical insight, man only wants platitudes. . . . The wall which I have raised around my existence I shall raise now a few feet higher."

Darwin answered to a remark in a letter from his friend Lyell relative to his theory of coral reefs: "Don't delude yourself with the thought that they will believe you before you have become as bald as I. As far as progress of opinion is concerned, I see distinctly that it will be extraordinarily slow . . . almost as slow as the modifications in species. I have begun to be tired of the storm of antagonistic dissensions."

This slowness in human progress and its constant interruption by reversion to crudeness and the uncivilized state, often raises the question of whether in general there is any such thing as human progress and whether it is to be expected that the human race ever will become reasonable.

CONCLUSIONS

A review of the phenomena of inert and living matter and of mind, ordinarily summarized as Nature, shows all of them produced by the interplay of the same energies.

The inquiry whether there is to be found an intimate relationship between the results of physico-chemical, biological scientific examination, leaves, as is tried to prove here, no doubt that the older dualistic explanation of the diverse phenomena observed, has to be dropped in favor of the monistic explanation. As far as differences of opinion among scientists still exist, they concern but details.

An *energetic* view of nature as a whole is the only way of getting a really satisfactory understanding of all the complex phenomena we observe. Continued scientific investigation has thrown light on the dark that has existed before and allowed us to bridge the gaps of our knowledge. Man's manifold cultural acquisitions, as e.g. domestication of animals, cultivation of plants, pottery, works in stone, bone, wood; the art of speaking, writing etc. were the initial steps. The development of imagination led in the course of time to reasonable behavior.

Intimate studies of mankind explain to us now, at an

age when the understanding of man became more imperative than ever before, how man can acquire his diverse faculties in the course of time. They give us hope that *even reason,* in the future may become a *common* attribute of the homo sapiens.

To be sure, in spite of man's success in bringing order into the flux of phenomena in many fields, cultural progress was achieved only by hard exertions during an enormous lapse of time. It was extremely slow, and often interrupted by reversions into crudity.

Man's ability to unfold his power over the environment to the degree of bringing order into social relations, of giving his life a higher value, creating a world where men could coexist in peace and security, has proved as yet insufficient to ward off disaster. In spite of all the preaching of reason and of lamenting its lack, man has never quite crossed the line separating barbarity from civilization. He has remained the slave of violence and passions, playing politics, abusing power, and behaving today still as irrationally as when John Stuart Mill called the human race: "a mixture of a few wise and many foolish individuals."

By recalling how quickly every single normal child learns to walk and to speak, we wonder why man does not cease to commit mistakes, builds castles in the air, has ever to start anew to solve the same unsolved problems, whilst his ever changing needs are raising new ones.

Observing how irrationally the bulk of human beings think and act, many of our contemporaries share the conclusions drawn by Hume: "that society's ills are uncurable, man's very nature renders reality intangible, real human progress does not exist and that the assumption that the human race on the whole will ever become reasonable is psychologically and logically indefensible."

However, all pessimism could never suppress the longing for immutable, self-evident, ultimate truth and the hope that sometime in the future it may be discovered.

"Man wants to know, and when he ceases to do so he is no longer a man." These words, that will be chiselled on the frieze of the new library in Carlston College, were once said by the distinguished scientist and statesman Fritjof Nansen.[65]

Moreover, man's success in shaping *laws of Nature* by building up general formulas abstracted from experience, holds the promise that he may one day also learn to master his mind in a similar way.

The thick wall of ignorance and prejudice behind which the bulk of human beings still have to live, renders them incapable of obtaining an adequate picture of the forces shaping destiny and of their own place in the scheme of things. Lacking this picture they are not able to build up theories fit to explode error nor can they arrive at a policy of handling practical social affairs with wisdom. Only by learning to recognize reality can they expect to foresee the future and to take the actions necessary to reach their longrange objectives.

Getting to the bottom of the problem of how human reason originates is by no means as senseless as many believe. Acquiring an insight into the laws of the mind is not a meaningless undertaking, but the only way to learn how to see things in the proper perspective and to exploit all possible ways of handling the day-to-day problems by mutual adjustment. It is the habit of practical men—including some politicians—to draw conclusions from isolated facts, to regard as real only what they can directly perceive with their senses, what they can see, touch, smell, hear and taste and to keep to discredited, unreliable ideas—conceptions originating from an age of ignorance—instead of accepting reason as guidance. They should mind Goethe's warning: "Do not scorn reason and science." Knowledge of the laws of BOTH, matter and mind, is needed to elevate human culture.

The knowledge of the laws of matter has been mis-used all too often to lower the level of culture. Thanks to mere technological progress we are now at the brink of disaster. To escape a catastrophe we must strive to understand the causes and consequences of events and spread this understanding. We cannot afford to look at world happenings like detached spectators watching a play in the theater which is of no personal concern to us. We must endeavor to shed light on the mysteries of the soul and try to gain an understanding of the origin of reason. Only knowledge of the WHOLE TRUTH will provide us with sufficiently dependable theories and enable us to base our actions on reason.

We cannot spare from reexamination many sanctified traditions such as religious beliefs nor can we retain them for the sole reason that they were established millenia ago.

As long as the nature of reason is a matter of controversy, discussion of the various views is necessary. Only COMPLETE INFORMATION of the trends underlying human history, without ambiguity, will enable every individual to form his opinion according to the facts and to act in a rational manner. Only if the facts are universally appreciated, can people accept the necessity of a sacrifice now so as to ward off a catastrophe in the future. Cut throat competition and hostile relations between nations may then be replaced by permanent cooperation.

GENIUS

INTRODUCTION

Any inquiry into the origin of genius and its accomplishments is frequently considered, even at this late date, as a fruitless waste of time.

Yet the rapidly increasing number of biographies dealing with men of genius, as well as the extensive monographs concerning genius, indicate that interest in this problem is increasing.

Two American scholars may be quoted to show to what extent the significance of the problem has been recognized in this country. "From the bare economic point of view the importance of geniuses is only beginning to be appreciated. . . . Where quality is the thing sought after, the thing supreme, quality is cheap, whatever be the price one has to pay for it." (William James.) "Let us find out how such golden eggs are laid and nurtured." (Terman, *Genetic Studies of Genius.* Stanford University Press, 1925.)

By means of a Rockefeller grant, investigations have been carried out recently on dogs, with a view to determining as precisely as possible the influence of heredity and environment. Being highly inbred and teachable, dogs appear to be particularly suited as test animals.

On the basis of his studies of the pertinent problems in the course of the past decades,[1] the author believes that the study of persons of genius is especially appropriate for anyone who wishes to shed light on connections that have so far remained obscure. Yet it was necessary to create the broadest possible foundation for these investigations, in order to obviate the danger of obtaining, instead of a permanently satisfactory framework, a useless

61

gathering of seemingly haphazard observations which, when viewed separately, may appear inessential. With this purpose in view, we have taken into consideration not only knowledge concerning nature in general and man in particular, but also all the manifold documents regarding manifestations of the mind as they are to be found in biographies, pathographies, diaries, memoirs, letters, confessions, and so on.

Data of especial value for the comprehension of the origin of superior achievements are contained in the autobiographies of men of genius. Therefore, the author has seen fit to let these men, as frequently as possible, speak for themselves.

Chapter I

1

DEFINITION OF THE CONCEPT "GENIUS"

EXAMPLES

What we mean when using the term "genius" may be explained most easily by pointing to the contexts in which it is generally used.

Themistocles was called a genius because he advised his compatriots to seek refuge on their ships before the approaching Persians. Rostopchin earned the same epithet by ordering Moscow set on fire. A discoverer is called a genius when he obtains, with the simplest means, such miraculous results as Faraday with an old bottle, or Newton with a prism, a lens, and a sheet of paper. The latter is said to have been inspired to his great discovery by nothing more than a falling apple; in a similar manner, Goethe was led to a great discovery by the sight of a sheep's skull, Pasteur by the observation of earthworms on a spot infested with anthrax, Priestley by the fact that a flaming piece of paper ceased to burn when lit over a fermenting liquid. John Ericsson, who through the invention of his *Monitor* prevented the recognition of the Confederates in Europe, was self-taught. Nor did lack of formal education prevent Charles Dickens from being, at the early age of 28, a popular writer.

The romanticists considered "genius": a dynamic spirit that no rules could hem in, one that no analysis or classification could ever fully explain. Genius, they maintained made its own rules and laws. Genius might be that of an individual person such as the artist, the writer or a Napoleon, mover of the world. It might be the genius of a people or a nation . . . an inherent national character making each people grow its own distinctive way which could be recognized only by a study of its history and not by rationalization.

Ranke's idea was, that: "Germans were destined to create the 'pure German State' corresponding to the genius of the nation . . ."

To Dr. Johnson the criterion of genius's eminence was: a man endowed with superior faculties.

Besides creative men who know how to reach their goal very quickly (we may mention here Justus Liebig and Carl Linné, whose teachings found recognition all over Europe within a few years), one also calls geniuses those who are distinguished by a capacity for fast production. Thus Haeckel wrote his "Generelle Morphologie" at one stretch, Nietzsche conceived the second part of "Zarathustra" very quickly . . . "conception was at once followed by birth." Voltaire finished his tragedy "Olympia" in six days, "Candide" in a few weeks and, when an acquaintance of his remarked after the performance of a "Pucelle" by another author: "you would have known how to use this material to better advantage," he jotted down—in rapid improvisation, within a few weeks—the first cantos of his own "Pucelle." Lord Byron's production was as fast "as my pen would write." "Lara I wrote while undressing when I came home from dances and fancy-balls in the frivolous year of 1818."

Goethe's "Iphigenia" was, in all its essential features, shaped in its first draft, "as if formed in one casting." Here is what he himself had to say about it. "This morning when I was riding over from Zento, I had the great good luck to invent (between sleeping and waking) a

64

limpid plan for "Iphigenia auf Delphos." There will be a fifth act, the likes of which cannot be often seen. I was happy like a child."

Of Theophile Gautier we are told that he wrote a flawless article at a desk at the printer's, without any preparation or any corrections of either form or contents, and Victor Hugo is said to have worked in the fashion of the Renaissance painters: surrounded by a flock of disciples and admirers. Rossini's "Don Juan" and "William Tell" were allegedly committed to paper at one stretch, in all the perfection of their classical form. Verdi needed only 40 days, so the story goes, to compose and orchestrate his "Rigoletto"; His biographers tell us that Mozart was able to write music "mechanically," on order, and without being at all influenced by moods. Rubens completed his "Adoration of the Kings" in two weeks, Tiepolo his "Twelve Apostles" in ten hours, and Rembrandt needed for the etching of an Amsterdam view less time than it took his servant to get some mustard from a neighborhood village.

The term "genius" is also used in the case of premature production, for instance with so-called child prodigies: such as the case of a young girl that at her first appearance on the stage did not show any sign of stage fright, the case of the daughter of the composer Dvorak, who is said to have played musical pieces at the tender age of 1½ years. Voltaire at the age of 10, and Frederike Boehmer, who died at the age of 15, were famous for their poems. Another phenomenon of this kind is the appearance of a valuable idea in a dream, or in a waking dream. It often appears at once in its most fitting form, as in the case of an actor who experiences his role before the actual performance, or of a painter who sees his picture, of a saint who sees his vision in a dream, with the dreamer's being aware of his own contribution. Strindberg tells us: "I believe in dreams, for my brain works sharpest when I sleep."

65

Rosegger wrote his folk drama "Am Tage des Gerichts" (On the day of judgment) immediately after awakening from a dream depicting a court scene; the composer Kienzl jotted down the final draft of his opera "Evangelimann" (The Gospel Man) "as though an invisible being led his hand: it was an outspoken compulsion."

"For once you are going to hear a dream," Richard Wagner wrote to Mathilde Wesendonk about "Tristan," "a dream that I have made sound. . . . I dreamt all this: never could my poor head have invented such a thing purposely."

What is true of the creative thoughts of the artist also holds good for those of the explorer. Herschel discovered the planet Uranus in a dream, as Leibnitz the basic idea of his world system, Duisberg the formula for an important dye, N. Bohr his atom model. Ehrlich first visualized the side-chain theory in a dream so that he was able, upon awakening, to write it down speedily without any changes. The German chemist Kekulé tells us an interesting story about his experience with dreams: "I was submerged in reveries. Before my eyes the atoms began to dance. I had always seen them in motion, those little beings, yet I had never succeeded in describing the manner of their motion. Today I saw how two smaller ones frequently joined as couples, how larger ones embraced two smaller ones, yet bigger ones held three or four of the small ones, and how all of them turned about in a whirling dance. The conductor's cry "Clapham Road!" woke me from my reveries, but I spent part of the night to commit sketches of these dream pictures to paper. This is how the "structure theory" came about. And something similar occurred in the case of the "benzol theory." . . . I was sitting in my study and writing a textbook, but I couldn't make any headway: my mind was on other things. I turned my chair toward the fireplace, and dozed off. Again the atoms danced before my eyes;

now my mind's eye distinguished larger formations, of manifold shapes; long rows, often more tightly joined. Everything was in motion, writhing and coiling in serpentine fashion, and lo and behold . . . what was this? one serpent grasped its own tail, and mockingly that thing whirled before my eyes . . . the benzol ring! Again I spent the rest of the night elaborating the consequences of the theory."

The different ways in which the term "genius" is used make it understandable that some consider fame as its most essential attribute,[2] while others set the greatest store by its accomplishments. It is largely in the latter sense that the term will be employed in the following deliberations. Many have asked themselves why it is that, among a number of individuals who all had the same opportunity to make a certain observation, only one succeeds in drawing the correct conclusions, or how it happens that an insight that has been long sought after in vain arises all of a sudden—at the moment of awakening, for instance—and as it were quite involuntarily?

"One ought to say: it thinks, in the same manner as one says: it lightens," essayist Lichtenberg once exclaimed. And the philosopher Edward Hartmann has stated: "Millions stare at the same phenomenon, and one genius finally grasps the concept."

2

GENIUS AND HEREDITY

The observed fact that a color grinder, a farmer, a craftsman, distinguished themselves later on in life as artists, scholars etc., as in the cases of Hunter, Owen, Burns, Caravaggio, Herschel, and also the frequent presence of mathematical, musical gifts, or a talent for draftsmanship, in the ascendence and descendence of certain families, have suggested the idea that we are dealing in such cases with an inherited disposition. The transference of a physical attribute, like the famous "Hapsburg lip," which the observer of the many existing portraits of members of that family can recognize through many generations, has been interpreted in the same manner. "All acts of genius are the work of instincts. If all the philosophers of the world had joined forces, they could never have created the "Armida" of Arnault." (Voltaire). And Goethe said: "Waer' nicht das Auge sonnenhaft, die Sonne koennt'es nicht erblicken." (Were not the eye sunlike itself, it never could perceive the sun.)

More recent authors also hold the same opinion. "The intuition of genius rests on hereditary substances of superior value, which intensify each other in their effect." (Sommer, the psychiatrist.) "Genius is of a pure race: of the fair type, and blond." (Hauser).

Yet many of the more recent authors no longer consider this explanation as incontestable as it had appeared to their predecessors. "Genius, as a matter of course, is based on hereditary disposition, and it cannot be substituted with effort. . . . However, which factor is decisive: the coupling of hereditary factors, the combined action of homonymous genes, or influences of divergent environmental conditions . . . we are as yet in no way able to determine." [3] Other authors show a similar degree of reticence. "The causes of the production of great men lie in a sphere wholly inaccessible to the social philosopher. He must simply accept geniuses as data just as Darwin accepts his spontaneous variations." (William James.) "The factors that lead to the accomplishments of genius are completely unknown." [4] "Although the attempt has been made for hundreds of years, no satisfactory answer has yet been given to the question as to what constitutes the essence of genius, and there is no chance that this answer will ever be given." [5]

The assumption that the possibilities for development are limited in the inherited disposition, that the talent of a child can be furthered by a summation of similar talents in the parents as well as by a partial dissimilarity of the transferred hereditary substances—this assumption, justified, must not lead to the seemingly logical conclusion that the much-admired sudden inspirations of genius, which illuminate like a lightning flash a situation that had remained obscure, are but a gift from Heaven, are nothing but a retarded remote effect of an extraordinary disposition.

In the field of electricity, the assumption of such a remote effect has long since been proved to be erroneous, and, we generally note that nature nowhere makes jumps.

The following facts are apt to support these theoretical reservations. Many geniuses do not show a trace of originality in their family trees. Apparently, what is being passed on by heredity is only a total of reactive possibilities, of tendencies and inclinations, of nervous and psychic excitability—(of the musical talent only some partial elements) —but not full-fledged qualities, convictions, judgments, diligence, character, acumen, imagination, firmness of purpose.

The achievements of one and the same genius differ vastly from each other. Together with outstanding achievements, we find performances that are mediocre, and even less than mediocre. Many geniuses had a hard time in school, and flunked their exams. Many failed in their earlier years to show any indication of the efficiency, the originality, the humor etc., which were to distinguish them later on. We refer to such men as Henry IV of France, Henry VI of England, Balzac, Turgenyev, Titian, Corot, Rembrandt, and many others. Alexander von Humboldt was advised to turn to a craft,

69

because he was so slow in the uptake. Yet he was only one of the many who were similarly misjudged. The fact that often even parents, teachers, classmates, and friends had no inkling of any special capabilities, must not be attributed to faulty observation only. In reporting the failure of Gregor Mendel to pass an examination for a teacher's position, his biographer states explicitly that at that time Mendel did not show any sign of a special talent.[6]

Noteworthy is also the manner in which men who had distinguished themselves by outstanding achievements judged their own talent. Darwin complained of a foggy memory; he calls himself awkward, a poor thinker, without the gift of quick grasp, without the ability to think in the abstract. "Anybody endowed with ordinary capabilities," he once said, "could have written my book if he had the patience and sufficient time. Whatever I may have achieved in science has been arrived at through long reflection, through diligence and patience. With such moderate abilities as I possess, it is truly surprising that I should have influenced, to a considerable extent, the belief of scientific men on some important points. . . . If I live to be eighty, I shall never cease to be amazed at finding myself a writer. Had somebody told me, that summer when I left, that by now I would be an angel, I should have considered that just as likely." [7]

In a similar vein John Stuart Mill said: "If I had been by nature extremely quick of apprehension, or had possessed a very accurate and retentive memory, or were of a remarkably active and energetic character, the trial would not be conclusive; but in all these natural gifts I am rather below than above par."

The assertion that pure races have been the true carriers of culture has proved to be untenable. Pure races are even less susceptible of improvement than mixed ones. The Nordic regions, which are said to be of pure race, have been particularly poor in geniuses and in

70

highly developed cultures; while, conversely, the culture of Italian High Renaissance was the product of a mixture of eminently gifted races. (Kretschmer.) A good disposition is as insufficient to make a lucky discoverer as good eyes are to make a lucky finder.

3

GENIUS AND ENVIRONMENT

As the recognition of the great significance of harmful environmental influences on the emergence of crime has forced a revision of the theory of the "born" criminal,[8] the demonstration of the importance of environmental factors for mental developments had compelled us to revise the theory of the "born" genius. (In this connection, the study of identical twins is almost as convincing as an experiment.)[9] No man remains the same in the course of his life: he changes. Environment is a co-factor in determining what road a man will take; whether he is going to be normal, or psychically ill, or a criminal. Environment influences a man's qualities, his character, his destiny, his future life: what he knows, what he can do, and what he wants to do.

Even as external a feature as the "mood for creation" is highly subject to the influence of environment. Tolstoy, Wagner, Ibsen, Wilhelm Busch were at their most productive in sunny spring weather. Spencer got his inspirations after breakfast, when his brain was rested. Gauss was at his best in the early morning, immediately after awakening. When Stendhal wrote "La Chartreuse de Parme" he found it useful to read every day one or two pages of the Code Civil. Goethe was not in a mood for anything whilst sitting: "whatever good results I find in my reflections come to me when I am walking."

Rousseau was never as prolific in thoughts as he was on trips that he made alone and on foot. Nietzsche wrote: "I can think and write only under the clearest sky, and when I feel a complete cheerfulness of mind and body ... Music now affords me sensations such as I have never before experienced, and every time an evening of music is followed by a morning of resolute insights and inspirations. It is as if I had bathed in a natural element."

Many a discovery seems merely accidental. A personal experience, a new method, an instrument, an idea, an experience that may be due to congenial working conditions, a passage in a book, an anecdote, a dream, a contest, even a measure of aggravation: all of them release inspiration. A mistaken assumption may lead to a discovery; thus, for instance, led the search for non-existing phlogiston to the discovery of oxygen; the search for cyanic ammonia resulted in the discovery of urea. A remark by an onlooker that the leg of the frog began to quiver every time the tip of the knife approached it, led to Galvani's discovery, and Nobel was guided toward the discovery of dynamite by the observation that nitro-glycerine oozing from a cracked glass vessel combined with packing material. A sample of gutta-percha, which had just been introduced at the time, helped Siemens invent a usable submarine cable; a remark by Siemens gave Reuter, who was then owner of a carrier pigeon service in Brussels, the idea to found the world famous news agency. The accidental fact that among eight mosquitoes examined one (coincidentally, the first one to be examined) showed positive findings afforded Sir Ronald Ross an insight into the development of malarial fever. According to a report in the New York Times, coincidence played a similar role in the discovery of penicillin. The Times quoted Sir Howard Florey, the co-discoverer: "In 1938 Dr. Chain and I decided that it would be profitable to make a systematic survey of naturally produced anti-bacterial substances.

Several hundred had to be examined. Fortunately, penicillin stood at the top of the list so that it was a matter of pure luck that its chemistry and biology were among the first to be studied."

Among earlier remarkable instances that demonstrate graphically the role of coincidence we quote: the solar eclipse, which aroused Tycho de Brahe's interest in astronomy and so kept it alive that, twelve years later, he was able to observe the sudden emergence of a star that had never been seen before and was conspicuous by its particularly strong luminosity; he proceeded to undertake the most precise measurings, which laid the foundation of his fame. Kepler, in turn, owed the possibility of his discovery to the lucky fact that, as Brahe's disciple, he assumed the exploration of the planet Mars, the only planet of an eccentricity sufficiently great to permit the demonstration—through the observation of its orbit—that planetary orbits are ellipses rather than circles. To a flock of parrots whose flight he could observe from his ship Columbus owed the insight that he would have to steer towards Southeast to find land. "The flight of birds decided the original distribution of the Romanic and Germanic groups of human beings." (Alexander v. Humboldt.) Darwin was very nearly deprived of his sea voyage when it seemed to the captain of the "Beagle" that the shape of his nose did not offer sufficient guaranties for his energy.

The cultural development of a nation as well as of the single individual is greatly influenced by space and time. "Physical factors—climate, diet, heat, soil—are of vital importance in the history of civilisation." (Ellsworth Huntington: "Mainsprings of Civilisation" and "Principles of Human Geography." 5th edition. John Wiley, Sons.)

Storms may become mental stimuli as much as a permanently cloudless sky. We may assume that it was the latter which led the Arabs to their early preoccupation with the world of stars. Space and time, also the forms of tradition, of political and social institutions make their influence felt in the failures as well as in the successes of the various generations, in the growing as in the disintegrating of civilizations. The specific qualities of space and time make the fervent mysticism of a man like Bernard de Clairvaux understandable as the outgrowth of the inner tension that he had in common with the entire twelfth century, just as the foundations of libraries and museums had turned Alexandria, Rhodes, and Pergamon into spiritual centers.

The following historic facts, too, find a similar explanation. The century of Euclid also produced the mathematicians Appolonius of Perga and Archimedes. The colonization of America coincides with the discovery of the sea route to India, with the first globe-circling voyage of Magellan, with the supreme blossoming of art and the revival of religious freedom. The epoch of the greatest discoveries in space and on the earth's surface was immediately followed by the conquest, by way of the telescope, of a considerable part of the ethereal space. The half century between the death of Kepler and Newton's discovery saw a whole series of great astronomical discoveries. The astronomical apparatus was greatly improved; the Academy of Science and the Paris Observatory were founded, and the margin of error in the accuracy of astronomical measurings, which in the days of Tycho de Brahe had still to be allowed for in arc-minutes, was now reduced to arc-seconds.

As soon as many men decide, at a certain historic juncture, to concern themselves with the problems of their time, it often happens that several scholars either solve the same problem simultaneously, though independently of each other, or solve parts of the problem in such a manner that these partial solutions complement each other. Thus, for instance, Leibnitz and Newton found the differential calculus at the same time. The law of energy was discovered by Robert Mayer, Joule, and Helmholtz simultaneously, as was the law of evolution by Darwin, Spencer, and Wallace. Oxygen was discovered at the same time by Scheele and Priestley. The idea to explain Kepler's laws by central forces inversely proportional to the square of the numbers occurred to several British scientists simultaneously. Other examples of simultaneous discovery: chloroform (Liebig and Sobeyron); glycogen (Hansen and Claude Bernard); the cause of puerperal fever (Semmelweis and O. Wendel Holmes); the TB bacillus (Robert Koch and Baumgarten), and so on. Independently of each other, several explorers clarified through their studies some problems important for the practical use of cocaine: Woehler tried to demonstrate and to prepare it, while others attempted to show that the chewing of coca leaves the tongue nerves numbed, that subcutaneous injection of cocaine made that part of the skin insensible, and that it and its derivates were highly usable in ophthalmology and surgery. The discovery of the so-called pancreas diabetes was due directly to the collaboration of Minkovsky, who contributed the idea, Mehring, who elaborated the operational technique and proposed to remove the pancreatic gland, and the laboratory assistant, who found sugar in the urine after the removal of the gland. After the cause of syphilis had been found, this discovery was speedily followed by that of the Wassermann reaction and that of the experimental transferability of the disease to apes and rabbits; the value of arsenic preparations for the treatment of the illness was also soon recognized.

Another environmental factor must be noted: the influence attributable to obscure artisans, painters, teachers,, etc. in the families of men of genius, or to the influence of father, mother, or wife, as in the cases of Mozart, Goethe, Mill.[10] Then there is the intercourse with great minds. "You have given me a second youth and you have made me a poet again, which I had almost ceased to be," Goethe wrote to Schiller. And Wagner said of his meeting with Liszt: "A storm of enthusiasm raged between us and thus we filled these eight days with so powerful a content that I am now, as it were, dazed by it."

The significance of example, of the model in the history of war, in politics, and science cannot be overlooked. Such attributes as love for music, passion for the theater, an inclination to observe patterns of regularity, can be transferred, as many examples show. Hippocrates served as a model for Aristotle, the Greek physicians for Boerhave, the founder of clinical teaching in medicine. An example that even the Bohemian nature of a father can be passed on to the son was the German poet and dramatist Wedekind.

The most usual means to incorporate the ideas of men of all ages into one's own, are books. Darwin writes from "The Beagle" to his teacher, Professor Henslow and later asks Professor Hooker to let Humboldt know that his entire career was the consequence of his reading Humboldt's "Narrative of Travels."[11] The reading of Pliny induced Himley, the physician, to recommend a medicament for the enlargement of the pupils; the "punctum saliens" (starting point) in the writings of Galen caused Harvey to discover the circulation of the blood.

Even the most original mind is apt to borrow from others, by profiting from their methods, ideas, and models. The uniqueness of an artist or a thinker consists merely in his ability to represent his time better than others.

Here is how Strindberg described the work of the poet, the procedure of the writer: "He takes an anecdote, told by another man over a glass of wine, he takes an episode out of a stranger's life; he takes the thoughts of philosophers, reports from newspapers, feelings out of his own imagination—and then he writes his little name under all this. . . . The poet does as the boas do: he covers his prey with slime, and then it belongs to him.

Beautiful webs he spins out of his own substance, so they say, yet nobody has seen how many he has sucked out first."

Greek and Roman culture did not arise by themselves; they are rooted in the cultures of Asia and Egypt. Just as the works of earlier bards were incorporated into the Odyssey, so the choruses of Aristophanes, disguised as reptiles, insects, or birds, are not of his own invention, even though we do not know his predecessors.

The artists of the Middle Ages have often taken over, without the slightest scruples, single figures as well as whole groups from the compositions of older masters. "These painters are not plagiarists, nor would it have occurred to one of them to consider the other as such. What they use is the common property of a school, produced by every one of them according to his lights, not in slavish imitation but in vital creation and with individually independent additions." This is what Jakob Burckhardt wrote about the school of Giotto. In works of sculpture we sometimes find a head, an arm or a leg inserted that stems from another artist. Thus the Louvre has besides the Venus of Arles a replica of that same statue with an antique head. Nor was that procedure unknown in the field of painting. A customary trick was the composition of a painting with details taken from various others. A forgery of a Dou picture was composed with material from three different works of that master.[12] Often the format was enlarged or reduced, nude figures were painted over, the breasts of a nursing mother covered with a piece of cloth. From Rubens' picture "Sine Cerere et Baccho friget Venus," (Without Ceres and Bacchus Venus freezes) the figure of Venus was cut away, and now the left half of the painting hangs in the Dresden Museum, while the right half has been combined with another left half, from the brush of another master and of an entirely different subject, to a new picture, a "Venus in Vulcan's forge."

77

Even the greatest artists have not disdained taking over parts of other men's work for their own purposes. Raphael, for instance, used motives of Michelangelo, and we can find in his work more than superficial parallels to Leonardo's "La Gioconda"; many a feature, as in the "Stanza di Heliodoro," is not even in invention his own.[13]

Shakespeare constructed the plot of his "Merchant of Venice" by fusing two tales he had found in the Gesta Romanorum: the lawsuit involving the pound of flesh, and the scene with the three caskets. The lines

> "His hemming and hawking, his expectorating
> You have succeeded in imitating,"

Schiller borrowed from Molière, who in turn had taken them from a Roman writer. For the description of the main figure in his "Beatrix," Balzac used a number of articles by Gautier verbatim. Goethe, in the lyrical poems of his earlier period, which are rightly counted among the most beautiful of all literature, clung almost slavishly to the models of Ovidius and Propertius. The chant of the holy anchoretes in the second part of "Faust" is but a poetical translation of a Pre-Renaissance painting, which he had seen on one of his trips.[14] Another example from Goethe's work is the folk poem "Heideroeslein," where his only alterations consisted in expert stylization. The lines

> Waer' es ein Gott, der nur von Aussen stiesse,
> im Kreis das All umlaufen liesse!
> Ihm ziemt die Welt des Innern zu bewegen.
> (Would he be God who only stirs from outside
> and makes the universe revolve around?
> Him it behooves to move the inner world)

is very nearly a translation of a passage by Giordano Bruno. The first sentence in "Faust":

78

Die Kunst ist lang
und kurz ist unser Leben
mir wird bei meinem kritischen Bestreben
doch oft in Kopf und Busen bang

(Art is long,
and brief is our life;
thus in my critical endeavors
I often tremble, both in head and heart)

is modelled after an aphorism of Hippocrates: Life is short, and art long; opportunity sleeping, experiment perilous, and judgment difficult. The second act of Goethe's "Clavigo" is taken almost word for word from Beaumarchais.

Without the careful investigations by literary scholars, hardly anyone would ever guess that all the following factors have contributed to the verses of Gretchen's prayer before the Mater Dolorosa, which speaks to our emotions like a cry from the sorrowful heart of a child: memories of the prophet Jeremiah, of a Stabat Mater, of the church songs of a medieval monk, Jacopone da Todi, of Renaissance pictures of the Virgin with a sword in her heart, and of the cantos of Ossian.[15]

Goethe did not in any way try to conceal these borrowings. "The greatest genius will never amount to anything if he wants to limit himself to his own resources, What would I be, what would remain of me, if this kind of appropriation were to endanger the quality of genius? What have I done? I have collected and used everything that I have seen, heard, observed. I have drawn upon the works of nature and of man. Every one of my writings has come to me through thousand different things. The scholar and the ignoramus, the wise man and the fool, childhood and old age have contributed their share. Without suspecting it, most of the time, they offered the gift of their thought, their abilities, their experiences. My work is a combination of beings taken from the

79

march of nature: the whole carries the name of Goethe
. . . Absurd Men! You act like certain philosophers, who
fancy that by shutting themselves up for thirty years in
their studies, or by doing nothing but sift and bolt the
ideas which they extract from their poor brains, they
would arrive at an inexhaustible source of originality.
Do you know what would come of that? Clouds, nothing
but clouds."

Nor are things different in music. Wagner confessed
that only the eight lines with which Hans Sachs is
greeted by the people in the last scene are taken from
his "Lied an Luther" (Song to Luther). "All the various
musical epochs show the same phenomenon," said Schu-
mann. "Bach, Händel, and Gluck, and later on Mozart,
Haydn, and Beethoven resemble each other so much in
hundreds of passages that one might easily take one for
the other." How much the librettist and the composer
borrow from the work of others we may show by the
following data concerning the origins of a work of art.
The study of these origins was facilitated by a rich
material of letters, diaries, newspaper clippings, original
texts, sketches, etc. contained in the "Zauberflöte" (Magic Flute) exhibition in Salzburg, 1928. From this material
we can easily find the general as well as the musical tendencies that participated in the origins of that opera.
Schikaneder's text contains many of the motives and elements then prevalent in literature and in the popular
theater. In the music, on the other hand, we find such
influences as that of the opera both buffa and seria, the
Singspiel, of the polyphonic church music of Händel
and Bach, of Gluck's operas, and finally of the finest
musical theorists of the 18th century, one of whom was
Mozart's father. . . . For the characteristic treatment of
the piccolo flute in the aria of Monostatos, the aria of
the Negro Amilkar was the model. The song of the three
and the threefold solemn call in the overture recall the
symbolism of the Masons. The "Hm, Hm" of Papageno,

the clown who was an almost indispensable feature of the plays of the time and whose feather suit we can find in the paintings of the time of Louis XIV, was an imitation of a comical realistic feature with which Philidor, in his "La Bucheronne," had represented the stammering of a mute person. Nor is the portrait aria original: love at the sight of a picture was a favorite theme of the time. The title itself was taken from "Lulo, or the magic flute," in the third volume of Wieland's "Dschindistan." Similar titles, such as "the magic knights," "the magic drum," "the magic bell" were all the rage. . . . Into the framing plot, based on the enmity between the radiant fairy and the evil sorcerer Bosphoro, (i.e., the Queen of the Night and Sarastro), new motives have been inserted under the influence of the Masonic ideology: the Egyptian milieu, and also the trials by fire and water, and the consecreation of the priest. The "three pages" delivered a pair of lovers already in "Monfalcone." The living model of Monostatos bore the name of Angelo Soliman; that of Sarastro was called Ignatz Born. If to all this we add the sharp competition that raged between the various Vienna theaters of the time, we have enumerated the most essential ones among the factors that participated in the creation of the "Magic Flute." The effect of that opera on posterity can be seen in the many new editions, new arrangements, and variations, which led already in 1793 a musical journal to complain: "This mozarting is never going to end!"

4

SHARE OF INDIVIDUAL EFFORT IN ACCOMPLISHMENTS OF GENIUS

Even where an optimum of disposition and the most favorable environmental conditions are present, a great work matures only if extraordinary efforts have been spent on it. The psychotherapeutist knows from experience that not even the simplest thought is transferred without effort. "The clear and calm communication of a factual datum, offered once, twice, or three times, while it is perceived is not appropriated by others, and thus remains without effect." (I. H. Schultz.)

Achievements that surpass the average in some way or another—as those of the businessman who, in difficult times, wants to maintain his position intact, or those of a man who has chosen an intellectual profession—make great claims on a person's working-power. The historian, for instance, cannot be satisfied with studying books on history, documents, letters, memoirs, and oral traditions, he has to supplement the testimony of other men—by preference of eyewitnesses, who are the best authorities —by scrutinizing such things as the inscriptions on coins and medals, the minutes of parliamentary discussions, and so on. The historian of literature, in addition to language, grammar, philosophy, and psychology, must take into consideration historical sources like manuscripts and old biographies and be able to evaluate the authenticity of the available texts. The archeologist must be informed about the originals as well as about a whole series of copies that are found on reliefs, coins, earthen vessels, cut stones . . . in short: about everything that may help explain the origins of works of art and craftsmanship. For the classification of fossil plants one needs the knowledge of the living as well as the fossil genera of plants and animals; geology and geography must assist the explorer in grouping his fossils according to time and place. And so on.

Even a merely exact rendition of a piece of music does not succeed without great devotion on the part of all participants. Any significant advance in technology is conquered by the work of generations. Any partial improvement, as for instance that aimed at the greater security, increased speed, and reduced cost of a transport system, requires a considerable exertion of human energy. This is equally true of the world of the book, radio, etc. Nor is a natural talent alone sufficient for anyone who wants to be an actor.

Any craft and any art must first be learned.

He who, in ancient Greece, wanted to gain influence on the masses, devoted the best years of his youth to the study of rhetorics, in order to become (as Burckhardt has remarked) at least a good speaker, if even only a mediocre politician. Charles Fox, the famous orator, who used to make a speech at least once every night, regretted—not without reason—that he had not done it more often. Even the born orator must first learn the art of speaking. Parnell, the Irishman, failed in his first attempt. Of William Pitt, undisputably the finest orator in the British House of Commons of his time, Macaulay said that "his first speech was just as empty and verbose as the maiden speeches of others."

The requirements for learning the art of painting are evidenced in the precepts that Leonardo established for his disciples. (According to Bandello, see Burghart's biography of Leonardo). "First, a young man must study the laws of perspective, for they are the measure of all things. Then, he must repeat the drawings of fine masters. Next, he must be able to draw from nature and to gain awareness of the foundation of what he has learned. After having dedicated some time to the contemplation of the works of different masters he must, ultimately, endeavor to employ what he has learned and to put it to practical use. . . . Draw a horse that drags his dead master and, behind him, make us see the traces of that dragging in the dust and in the mud. The beaten and vanquished men make pale, with brows raised and knitted, and let the skin above the brows be drawn in many folds, expressing sorrow. Beside the nose, several furrows are to be inserted, radiating arcwise from the nostrils to the corners of the eyes . . . and if you show the horses racing away from the turmoil, then place the little clouds of dust which they kick up in such distance from each other that they correspond to the leaps of the horses, and make them, the farther they remain behind the horse, the higher and thinner, and the more drawn-out."

In order to become no more than a good novelist one needs, according to Nietzsche, no less than the following: "Let him travel like a landscape painter and costume designer; let him excerpt from various sciences whatever makes an artistic effect when it is only well represented. Let him, finally, ponder over the motives of human acts and let him not disdain any hints that might inform him on that topic: by day and by night he ought to be a collector of such things. In such manifold exercises let him spend some ten years; what he then creates in his workshop may well venture into the light of the street. . . . What, however, are most of them doing? They start, not with a part, but with the whole. True, occasionally they may get a lucky break and attract attention; yet their breaks are bound to become less and less lucky, and for sound, comprehensible reasons."

The man who undertakes to become the founder of a great industrial enterprise, or to raise himself to the stature of a great statesman, strategist, or scholar, must be prepared to meet with great difficulties. To give the right answers to the questions at hand, to draw the correct conclusions, to detect a grain of truth: all this one does not, as a rule, succeed in doing without an uncommon degree of mental effort even in those cases where it might seem as if these achievements had, so to speak, accomplished themselves automatically. Before our first thoughts can be turned into the best possible thoughts, and before the sharply outlined shape of a fruitful idea crystallizes out of the chaos of incoherent flashes of insight, many nebulosities, prejudices, and contradictions, which obstruct the path to a new idea, must be removed. How great an effort it takes to formulate clearly a new idea, even after it has been found, we may learn from a remark of Laplace, who once said that, whenever he began a sentence with the words "it is evident," he realized that he had many hours of hard work before him.

Even the effort required of an artist who does not aspire to saying anything essentially new but only wants to clothe an old truth in a new attire is an immense one. Flaubert is said to have taken two days to write two lines. In order to be sure that the idiomatic remarks of his figures were couched in the style of the time he was describing, he leafed through many issues of the magazine Charivari; he spent weeks going over collections of engravings to obtain information on costumes and postures of earlier generations; in order to be able to write the thirty pages on agriculture in his "Bouvard et Pecuchet," he studied 101 different works, and for the study of the Salammbo milieu he made a special trip to Tunis and Carthage.

Balzac worked for eighteen hours at a stretch, even while he ate, in the following fashion: "The first draft is put down with great gaps between the single paragraphs and the enormously wide margins are filled in gradually, until the entire sheet, with its upward and downward radii, its tangential lines, etc. resembles the picture of a firework." "On every sheet, he used only 8-10 lines, because he lacks sureness of expression and is unable to find at once the definitive formulation. Whereas at first he has only the skeleton of a novel ready, the details are invented by and by. Half of his remuneration is spent on the correction of proofs."

That efforts of this kind are by no means superfluous becomes clear when we learn, from Benjamin Constant for instance, that he had filled such piles of paper as to have lost any system of finding anything in his own notes. An expert on Heine wrote: "Never have I seen a manuscript as rich in corrections as the one of 'Atta Troll' in the Royal Academy of Berlin." In Heine's more extensive literary creations, it is said, every line has been done over time and again. Another author said of himself: "I put down one and the same line and one and the same occurrence five to eight to twelve times, until I arrive at the greatest possible precision. My conviction of the insufficiency of each current version is based purely on feelings."

This particular kind of procedure is by no means exceptional: Spencer remodelled his "System of Sociology" five times, Buffon his work eleven times. Nietzsche sometimes rewrote his text fifteen times; Gibbon as many as nineteen times. On occasion, Dostoievsky went over a piece of writing ten times again, and was even then dissatisfied with his work. "I do not want," he once said, "to write under the compulsion of a deadline; I want to do things as Tolstoy, Turgenev, and Goncharov did. At least one work of mine must be written freely and without the fetters of a fixed deadline." Ibsen, too, was in the habit of rewriting his manuscripts, until they lay before him in fair copy, without any corrections.

In order to gain a conception of the scope of the effort required, we might remember the great share which youthful impressions often have in subsequent successes. The entire "Barber of Seville" is foreshadowed in Rossini's early opera "La scala di sete." Columbus had been deeply impressed by a passage in the book "Imago mundi," Kepler by a passage in Plato, Schliemann, the discoverer of ancient Troy, by the reading of Homer. Goethe avowed: "Ever since I was a youth, it has been my urge and my torment to learn to know, in its most varied forms, all that is commonly human as it is spread over the globe." Fifty years he devoted to the exploration of nature. Darwin said: "From earliest childhood on I have had the strongest desire to understand and to comprehend whatever I observed." He was prepared to ponder any number of years over an unsettled problem. "My diligence in observing and gathering facts has been as great as it possibly could be." Newton published his work twenty years after its inception. It took Bergius the same number of years to produce alcohol and dextrose from wood. Marconi hardly took time out to eat. Schiller carried his "Lied von der Glocke" (Song of the Bell) in him for a whole year before setting it forth. Others, Goethe among them, sometimes put a work aside to resume it years later.

Therefore it hardly seems accidental that the greatest literary creations—Don Quixote, Gil Blas, Robinson Crusoe, Gulliver's Travels—were the works of authors advanced in years.[16]

The following report of a surgeon shows how manifold are the studies—of the pertinent literature as well as of the findings in the laboratory, the clinic, the operation and dissection rooms—that precede the discovery of a new syndrome: "At first, like all observers who had confined themselves to microscopic examination only, I could not explain this bleeding. This, however, did not prevent me from making careful notes, without any preconceived notions, of every detail of the operation findings, even though they may have seemed unimportant at the moment. Thus I was able to make valuable use of notes concerning the first, obscure cases later on when they had become clearer to me in the light of positive findings obtained by that time. . . . When exploring the picture of a new disease I consider it impermissible to pass lightly over positive anatomical findings, even if they are of minor significance and their relation to the symptoms are not immediately obvious. I consider it equally impermissible to draw the conclusion—from whatever small part of the changes is visible to our eyes, even if armed with instruments—that all the rest that does not appear diseased to us is indeed healthy. Quite the contrary; wherever microscopic examination is lacking, we are forced as well as justified to combine and complement, on the ground of our anatomo-pathological experience, those fragments of the pathological changes to which our perception is limited. In collecting and sifting them, we shall arrive at well-founded concepts as to the anatomical basis of the symptoms."[17]

All these observations would seem to indicate that it is the honesty of the effort that makes the great explorer, the great artist. In the light of this concept it appears almost a matter of course that an artist whose working power (as in the cases of Michelangelo, Leonardo and others) is sufficient to embrace equally architecture, painting, and plastic art, occasionally will be enabled to see well-known things under a new light. The same goes for the scientist who, comprising in his person a multifarious knowledge, is in a position to view a datum from various different angles. This, for instance, was the way in which the chemist Justus Liebig looked at biological problems, Helmholtz, the physicist, at medical, and Billroth, a man well versed in pathological anatomy, at surgical problems.

Phenomena such as precocity, the ability to produce with uncommon speed, and ideas that seem to emerge independently ("intuitions"), are only seemingly contradictions to the above contention that honesty of effort is the decisive factor. Pre-maturity develops under the influence of a special environment. Thus Auguste Boehmer belonged to the circle of Goethe and Schiller in Weimar; Voltaire, when still a child, lived in a society that counted a number of oustanding minds among its members. Nor did he really produce as quickly as has been claimed. His "Pucelle" he published 32 years after he first conceived it; to his "History of the Time of Louis XIV" he added corrections over a stretch of twenty years. Before completing his "Candide" he locked himself up for three days and opened the door only to take in his meals and coffee. On his "Mohammed" he consulted for years with all his acquaintances, both male and female, he removed objectionable passages, and added others; he listened patiently to all the arguments of the actors; he tried to find out how he could—in the most considerate manner possible—pile up the horrors of the plot and provoke pity in the hearts of the audience. The main scenes of his plays he tried out as a builder tests the bearing capacity of his beams. The variants contained in the definitive edition of his tragedy "Irene" take up no less than seven pages in small print: that work had been revised, improved, rewritten time and again.

Other cases supply us with similar data. As regards Lord Byron, it is true enough that he slept during daytime; but he rose after sundown, and for months on end he spent every night writing. About the preparations for Goethe's "Iphigenia," a great expert like Kuno Fischer has this to say: "How long Goethe pondered over the subject-matter of "Iphigenia" and over his own interpretation of it, before he proceeded to the actual execution of his work, we do not know. In life as well as in poetic creation such perfection of the soul ripens only by degrees . . . The first prose version had taken up six weeks; it took him four months to complete the final metric version. The homeland of the creative formation (of this work) was Goethe's garden house, the Schwalbenstein, and Weimar; the homeland of its ultimate completion was the Lake of Garda, Verona, Vicenza, Venice, Bologna, and Rome."

As little as the abilities already mentioned does the capacity for inspiration derive from super-sensual powers, even though it is true that the one who has such inspirations may not know how he got by them. The much-admired "diagnosis at first sight" of the doctor is no more an initial phenomenon than is the melodic inspiration of the musician. Both are much rather a late link, and the climax, in the chain of steady diligent effort.[18]

Only the experienced physician will be able to pronounce the diagnosis "diabetes" at once upon entering a sickroom, because in him the perception of an aceton smell recalls (without any further consideration, as it were below the threshold of consciousness) well-known symptoms that complement the picture of diabetes. That a musician who enjoys writing because it is for him so to say the thing he likes more than anything else gets most of his ideas in a steady surge, just by playing, is documented in an obituary that Arnold Schönberg dedicated to George Gershwin. "Music to him was the air he breathed, the food which nourished him, the drink that refreshed him. Music was what made him feel and music was the feeling he expressed." [19]

The elements from which inspiration arises "suddenly" enter into relation to each other only gradually. Such unverifiable tales as the one that the observation of a falling apple sufficed for Newton to find his famous law gravely distort the real state of affairs and are apt to support the erroneous belief that intuition originates all of a sudden. Yet the idea that the moon would tumble down to the earth if it were not held suspended by centrifugal forces emerged in ancient times already, nor would Newton have been able to solve the problem that had occupied him for a long time (he had been compelled to set it aside for seventeen years) had a recently published work by the physicist Pickard on the measuring by degrees not made it possible for him to supply mathematical proof. Now, as with one single stroke, a relation could be established between such different partial results of earlier exploration as: the elliptic shape of planetary orbits, the advance of the equinoxes, low tide and high tide, etc. Goethe has told us how he found the inspiration for his "The Sorrows of Werther": "I was collecting elements that had been floating within me for a number of years. I endeavored to retain a vivid picture of the cases that had been most urgent and most frightening to me. Yet nothing would take shape. What was lacking was an occasion in which they (these elements) could be embodied. All of a sudden, I hear the news of Jerusalem's death, and immediately after the general rumor the most precise circumstantial description . . . (and my idea took shape) like water in a vessel, which, on the freezing point, turns into ice at the slightest shock."

Chapter II

1

THE SIGNIFICANCE OF REPETITION

In the crystallization of intuition the opportunity for repetition, for the thinking-out of a given subject, plays a considerable part. "I need to see many women that are beautiful: then the picture of a single one takes shape in my mind" (Raphael to Count Castiglione). The title part in Raimund's Viennese comedy "Der Verschwender" (The Wastrel) was patterned from the model of many a rich man who fell victim to temptation. One has to see many abnormal human beings before the question arises: what is the norm? Only after having looked at many tamed animals does one ask: what is domestication? It was only because he had been searching for a good cable insulator for a long time that Siemens was at once prepared to test gutta-percha when it was suggested to him. When Galvani was prodded to attempt extensive investigations by the remark of a spectator at his experiments that the frog leg began quivering with every approach of the tip of the knife, the reason was that he had long suspected the existence of animal electricity.

It is by no means surprising that the significant role of repetition in the struggle for success should have occurred to the discoverers time and again. Columbus wrote: "Every time when I am sailing from Spain to India, I find, as soon as I arrive 100 miles West of the Azores, an extraordinary change in the movements of the celestial bodies, in the temperature of the air, and in the condition of the ocean. I have observed these changes carefully and have noted that the sea compasses that, until then, had shown a declination toward North-East now moved toward North-West." [20]

Darwin offers another example. "Fifteen months after my systematic studies had begun, I happened to read Malthus' essay "On Population." Since I was sufficiently prepared, mainly by my continued observation of the living habits of animals and plants, to appreciate the ever-present struggle for existence, the idea occurred to me at once that under such conditions favorable deviations would have a tendency to be preserved, unfavorable ones to be destroyed. The result would be the formation of new species. . . . Here I had a theory with which I could work." On another occasion he wrote: "It took an accidental repetition of an observation" (to put him on the track of another idea); "I was amazed by the manner in which, as you moved southward on the continent, closely related animals replace each other. On my way back, I repeated the observation of the specifically South American character of the animals on the islands of the Galapagos Archipelago, in particular of the manner in which they deviate from each other on every one of these islands, which all belong to the same group . . .", and now the thought matured in his mind that the numerous observable deviations within the fauna and flora of these islands, which obviously had risen from the ocean only recently, might be attributable to the assimilation of the animals and plants of the nearby mainland to the living conditions newly imposed on them.—One more phenomenon that struck him after repeated observation only was the one that seedlings originating from auto-impregnation are inferior to those obtained through cross-impregnation.

John Stuart Mill, too, was aware of the significance

of repetition: he fully realized the evil use to which axioms may be put in the drawing of conclusions only as he was reading a certain sentence for the second time.

A collision of railroad trains set Westinghouse to thinking about the construction of instruments for the prevention of such accidents. This first occasion, however, merely pointed to the direction in which his thoughts would have to move. Before he conceived his plan for a reliable brake, which was to win him fame, he had to witness a second train collision, in which the two engineers, although fully aware of the danger, proved impotent to prevent the disaster, owing to the lack of any efficient instrument.

The experiences of animal tamers point to the fact that, in the intuitive grasping of a situation, the significance of repetition is a similar one in the animal kingdom as it is for man. For instance, before a seal carrying a torch in his mouth can be induced to throw that torch up into the air so that it will whirl around and then to catch it again (a task that he will master either not at all or, suddenly, all at once), the tamer must have spent months of enormous patience in showing the experiment to the animal with a simple wooden stick.[21]

Every new repetition of a complicated situation finds the brain better prepared than on the previous occasion, thanks to preceding attempts at grasping the connections. An insignificant circumstance, unobserved on the first occasion, or possibly not even present at that time, may then suffice to release intuition. The importance of the subconscious thought process that follows the first emergence of a situation is easily overlooked. Yet it contributes to the appearance of intuition in the same fashion as do the thought processes during sleep and dream. "The subconscious mind has its own preoccupations, literally simple ideas on which it ruminates." Balzac offers this example of self-observation: "Even when I sleep I do not cease working. For I reserve the decision on certain literary difficulties until after awakening and, upon awakening, I find that these decisions have been taken. Consequently, my brain works while I sleep."

Our daytime preoccupations follow us into our sleep and dream. The dream world that holds us engulfed during the day gives no surcease even at night.

2

THE SIGNIFICANCE OF CONSTANCY OF PURPOSE

Yet this "repetition of opportunity" does not endow just everybody and anybody with a gift for the gradual penetration into the depth of things that is the prerequisite for the attainment of the specialized knowledge and ability needed in the solution of intricate problems. That hothouse atmosphere in which intuitions thrive particularly is found only in the consciousness of a very special, sharply characterized group of men: it is found only in those "who are so absorbed by a problem that it drives them towards their specific goal and makes them use their forces to the utmost," while for the common run of men the probing into a given question does not reach beyond the layer of generally human interests. In men belonging to that special group we note that they have hardly any interests beyond those of their calling. In order to write a book, they are prepared to turn over half a library, like Samuel Johnson.[22] We know of inventors that their minds have been on their particular goals from the days of their youth, as with Ericson or Bessemer; the same is true of such painters as Leonardo, Reynolds, Hogarth. The latter used to be so engrossed with his work that, when the worst came to the worst,

95

he would go on making pencil sketches on the nail of his left thumb. Bach, we are told, showed a similar stubbornness in the pursuit of his musical studies: when they took his candle away he went on working by the light of the moon.

No barrier remains insurmountable for those whose passion is genuine, and not merely a passing fad, for those that are concerned with nothing but their great idea, to which for them all else is related. Once they have grasped their problem, their thoughts begin to revolve around it and they return to it again and again. Their problem follows them wherever they go, and does not release them even in company. H. Spencer confessed: "As regards my thoughts, it takes nothing to have them, everything to get rid of them; when I want to get rid of them I find it devilishly hard." In a similar fashion Siemens said: "I have never been able to repress completely the thoughts and plans that were on my mind at a given time."

After one has pursued a thought intensively for a long time, that thought in the end becomes itself the pursuer. Once obsessed by a thought a man becomes entirely "onesided." Such men are comparable to a red glass that permits only red light to penetrate while it reflects all others. Sometimes such a person may appear eccentric, as did Balzac when he interrupted an acquaintance, who told him of his sister's illness, with the remark: "all this is well and good, but let's turn now to reality and talk about Eugenie Grandet (the heroine in Balzac's novel of the same name)."

However, this "one-sidedness" is often the source of constancy of purpose and thus of great successes. History has innumerable such examples. So it is told of Vesalius, that already when in school, he dissected mice, moles, cats and dogs, even succeeded in obtaining a human skeleton by robbing a gibbet. His family had produced already five generations of physicians, his teacher's Sylvius text book was acknowledged as learned and competent. In his book "Fabrica" Vesalius continued in the best spirit of his time, in the direction set by Carpa and Massa.[23] Constantine the Great was prepared to bring every sacrifice to his passion to become the sole ruler of the Roman Empire: he was willing to have his son, his wife, and many members of his family murdered. Philip of Macedon, too, belonged to this type of man. Of him Demosthenes has told us: "to gain empire and power he had an eye knocked out, his collar bone broken, his arm and his legs maimed; he abandoned to Fortune any part of his body she cared to take so that honor and glory might be the portion of the rest." Also Charles XII of Sweden, who had his mind set on dethroning the king of Poland, even though he should have to spend 150 years in the process. Lenin said of himself: "There is no other man who is absorbed by the revolution 24 hours a day, who has no other thought but the thought of revolution and who even when he sleeps dreams nothing but revolution." [24] Jakob Burckhardt called Rembrandt "one of the one-sided ones, who represent one single capacity almost exclusively yet with an unheard-of power."

Occasionally it is not this concentration so much that strikes us as it is the absorption and absent-mindedness ensuing from it, as in the case of the abbot Bernard de Clairvaux who, after having spent a whole day riding alongside the Lake of Geneva, when asked how he liked the lake answered he was not aware of any lake.

There are many instances to show how unpredictable are the ways that may lead to a discovery if only "constancy of purpose" is not lacking. The alchemists, who had been searching eternal youth, the philosopher's stone and the art of making gold, found none of these; yet they did find such methods and apparatus as the craft of distillation, the chemical retort, the crucible, and medicaments such as opium, quicksilver, antimony, bismuth, zinc, Glauber's salt, and so on. Kepler arrived at his miraculous laws by deliberations of a kind that caused one author to exclaim: "He made his discoveries like a blind man who uses a stick to find his way."

3

THE MOTIVES FOR CONSTANCY OF PURPOSE

Since hereditary disposition, environment, and individual effort participate in the mental make-up of every human being, one other explanation becomes imperative: how does it happen that the concomitant action of these factors, even under seemingly similar conditions, provokes only a few individuals to superior achievements, while in the majority it results only in amateurish activities, or in a nervous, possibly psychotic disposition, or even in criminal attitudes?

We are tempted to inquire into the stimuli that cause one man to be susceptible to beauty, another one to bad weather, to atmospheric influences such as electricity in the air; a third one develops an irresistible personality, radiating suggestive power, while yet another "has the penetration to seize relationship of facts and principles and to reduce them to novel and concrete combinations," and thus ultimately proceeds from unformed matter to clearly outlined concepts, from non-knowledge to cognition, from the lack of a craft to the fullness of art, from the non-fitting to the fitting.

Biographies—particularly those of a "confessional" nature—supply us with many a useful hint regarding the stimuli by which individuals are motivated and by which, occasionally, the quality of genius is released. 'I know of no entertainment but that provided me by my head. Reading and writing are as important to me as eating and drinking." (Lichtenberg). "S'occuper c'est savoir jouir" (to occupy oneself is to know how to enjoy oneself) (Voltaire). "When I cannot create songs or poems, life is no longer life for me." (Tasso). "I keep on composing as though for all the rest of my life I never wanted to work on anything else any more. I am so inseparably welded to this work that I could willingly sacrifice my life . . . What am I without my work!" (Richard Wagner). "Nothing but my mood and my inclination toward perseveration will tell me whether something is possible for me; impossible is only what I no longer feel like doing." (Schopenhauer)

When Karl Ernest Baer, the naturalist, saw—the first man ever to see that sight—a human egg under a microscope, he had to compose himself first before daring to have a second look . . . Goethe once said: "I am so overjoyed that all my entrails are stirring. I have found neither gold nor silver, yet something that gives me unspeakable joy, the os maxillare (maxillary bone) in man. I compared the skull of man and animal, came upon the right track, and lo and behold: the keystone of man was not missing—there it was!"

The pleasure accompanying the scientist's and the artist's every smallest progress inspires him to continue his work. Thus we see also the inventor hunt after his good luck along the roads he has found to be the right ones always eager to intensify his "elan vital," if possible to point of ecstasy. John Ericson, we are told, was fascinated by machines at an age when other children play with toys.

Nor does the born soldier feel differently about this, as we may learn from a description by the Prince de Ligne: "If your dreams are not filled with the soldier's profession, if you don't devour books about war and maps of the places where they were fought, if you don't kiss the roads that old soldiers have trod and don't cry when you listen to their tales of battle, if you don't die for longing to emulate them and for shame not to have seen what they have seen, even though that is hardly your fault—then throw away your uniform: you are a disgrace to it. If having fought in one single battle does not throw you into a state of ecstasy, if you don't feel the desire to fight in all of them, if you are absent-minded, if the thought that rain might prevent your regiment from going on manoeuver does not make you tremble, then yield your place to a young man who is the way I require him to be."

Yet stimuli for an extraordinary achievement can also be derived from everything that makes our pulses beat faster, from all the circumstances that tend to remove a deep depression, to offer release from annoying tension. Any loss that asks to be replaced, any peril to which our instinct for self-preservation may be exposed, everything that upsets our mental equilibrium can lead to endeavors to reconquer the latter, and even to an entirely revised attitude towards life. Critical situations, grave impairments of our vital interests, illness, mutilation, defects of body and soul: all these can act in this fashion.

The immediate cause for the conversion of St. Ignatius was a crippling injury. What led to the foundation of the house of Plantin, a family prominent for centuries in the art of book-printing, was an assault which forced the founder to give up his original craft of bookbinding. In pondering over his long illness, Nietzsche wrote: "do I not owe to it infinitely more than to my health? I do indeed owe to it a higher kind of health; I owe it my philosophy. Great pain is the great deliverer . . . Now I have for the first time cast my main ideas into a mold, and behold: in so doing, I have most likely given form also to myself."

As the lack of an appropriate calculating system induced Newton to invent the differential calculus, so a shortage of human material led Traube and Koch to turn to animal experiments. The desire to prove his descendance from kings inspired Count Gobineau to formulate his racial theory. Not infrequently do we find a craving for the re-establishment of a lost mental equilibrium expressed in confessions of great men, St. Augustin, for instance, or J. J. Rousseau. The confessions of the latter have been called, because of the hallucinations referred to in that book, "the defense of a paranoic." Another example is that of Schopenhauer, a neurotic who suffered from obsessions. The book of the notorious Marquis de Sade allegedly had no other purpose but to justify the abnormality which bears his name. As typical of such a state of mind we quote a passage from a letter that the great misogynist Strindberg wrote to his friend Heidenstamm: "Do you really understand my hatred for women, which is but the obverse of my horrifying desire for the opposite sex? If I faint in my sleep and bite my tongue: all this is only the consequence of my celibacy."

Once we begin to pay attention to these connections, we find them to be more frequent than we might have expected. A case in point is Tolstoy who, after a youth of gambling and debauch, underwent a strange transformation. "The artist Tolstoy emerged late, not until he had indulged for years in a brutish promiscuity, which preyed upon his conscience all his life. 'Sensuality tortures me,' he said. With the self-expression he found in writing came an intense preoccupation with self-criticism, with a search for truth and for God. . . . It was moral perfection for which Tolstoy craved so hungrily."[25]

In this connection, it may be interesting to quote from an introduction to "Tales and Poems of Mystery and Imagination"[26] by E. A. Poe, where it is said that the substance of that writer's creation was nothing but "man's loneliness, man's hopelessness . . . reflections of the griefs, ambitions and disappointments of his youth."

Even behind works like Goethe's "Iphigenia," "Wilhelm Meister," or "Tasso," or the creations of some natural scientists, works which appear so perfect and serene that one might be inclined to assume they were created in complete peace of mind, one discovers, as soon as one probes into the history of their origins, a substratum of deepest emotion.

Only he who feels compelled to gather all his available strength in the battle for the great goal he is pursuing will also have that courage of his own convictions which is indispensable in any attempt at blazing trails for new ideas. The very fact of the "availability" of the old, accepted ideas has a retarding effect, since it supports a generally prevailing inclination to prefer a contemplative life to the exploration of truth, to the introduction of new and thorough reforms, and so on. The presence of strong stimuli is a precondition for any heroic endeavor.

Chapter III

1

GENIUS AND PSYCHOPATHY

Among these stimuli, the ones induced by an abnormal psychic condition are of especial importance. Some scholars have tried to link the origins of genius and its achievements with the presence of anatomical changes in the brain; for instance, the genius of Helmholtz with a congenital hydrocephalus, which supposedly was the cause of his permanent intelligence.[27] A considerably greater sensation, however, was provoked by the assertion of a number of psychiatrists to the effect that there exists a regular inter-relation between the abnormal accomplishment and an abnormal mental condition. One author writes: "It may be embarrassing, but in time to come we shall have to take note of the fact that many a man became a genius by acquiring a disease." Lange-Eichbaum estimates [29] that nine tenths of all geniuses are abnormal. According to him, practically all geniuses are psychopaths: the healthy person is simply unable to accomplish what mankind is longing for. "Genius is not harmonic, but nervous, with a tendency for psychic difficulties, even if not actually demented; psychotic, or showing a disposition toward psychosis, and degenerated. The problem of genius is full of profound obscurities and harsh question marks, a problem that has stirred in the brains of men for centuries and is still disquieting the finest thinkers." . . .

103

Kretschmer does not see in genius the ideal picture of a harmonic man, brimful with health, endowed with the highest intelligence, imagination, originality, creative urge, superior to other men in every respect, a man who is in no need of rules, knowledge, or work, in order to solve intuitively the most complicated problems. Much rather does he believe that there exist considerable biological connections between genius and the realm of psychopathic degeneration. "This constantly recurrent partial element of genius, far from being a regrettable external necessity, is an indispensable and essential component of the quality of genius in the narrower sense of the term. . . . Men as gifted as Nietzsche imagined them have never existed. . . . The combination of supreme health with supreme genius, as envisaged by Nietzsche, does not exist."

If we look over the long list of personalities whom Lange-Eichbaum and Kretschmer have called either psychotic or psychopathic, we indeed gain the impression that genius and mental health are found only rarely in co-existence.

Opinions differ as yet very widely as to the inner connections between genius and psychopathy. Whereas Paul Schroeder claims "proof is overwhelming, the connection a fact," Buergi[30] states: "Great artists are usually strong and healthy, both physically and mentally," and Birnbaum: "Genius is not degeneration, nor is it psychopathic; its essence has not yet been grasped." A similar view is taken by Luxemburger.[31] Psychopathy, he says, is a term of many meanings, one easily misunderstood. The great majority of psychopaths can be interpreted only on the basis of characterological studies. In his opinion, there is no such thing as psychopathic symptoms proper, nor are psychopaths really ill: "To conceive of all psychopaths as of pathological cases must lead, in practice, to fallacious conclusions; to force all of them as abortive cases into the Procrustes bed of psychosis would mean to misunderstand them thoroughly, on medical as well as on sociological grounds. . . . What is usually subsumed under such terms as disharmonic, psychopathic etc., has its various roots in the characterological and the pathological strata. The assumption that the disposition of genius depends on the presence of degeneration features in the hereditary substance I consider a fallacy derived from biased casuistry."

O. Vogt, of the Kaiser Wilhelm Institut in Berlin, explains the co-appearance of the above nervous peculiarities and defects with special talents by a simultaneous over-and under-development of certain centers, which is caused by the limitation of space available to the brain as a whole. He sees the future evolution in the development, not of universal geniuses, but of special talents. Alfred Adler explains the achievements of genius as due to "excessive efforts to acquire prestige and power by cultivating existing one-sided abilities, and thereby to over-compensate a perceived insufficiency."

In this manner, Adler believes, Beethoven's work was intended to help overcome the insecurity caused by his deafness.

Gilbert Clarke in his book: "Shelley and Byron" is writing: "Deformed—Transformed," Byron's tragedy, is by far the most self-revealing of all his poems, inasmuch as it disclosed how deeply the sense of his physical deformity preyed upon his sensitive mind and how fiercely it had stimulated his ambition to achieve heights which were denied to the perfection of form.

In order to make up our minds as to which of these widely divergent judgments we are to trust in, we want to ask this preliminary question: what are the characteristics of psychopathy? According to Lange-Eichbaum, the psychopath is, on the whole, undoubtedly less reasonable than the average person, he yields more readily to momentary impulses, his affects carry away his rea-

105

son, he endangers his offspring . . . the descendants often degenerate because they inherit the father's psychopathic disposition. Proof of the pathological character of psychopathy are those cases which border on psychosis. To a certain extent, the psychopath is unfitted for life, and his biologically negative components may be intensified in his offspring. Although the psychopath does not show any characteristics that are not at least potentially present in normal persons too, he is nevertheless conspicuous by such qualities as: inattention, absent-mindedness, absorption, irritability, malice, spite, stubbornness, unpredictability, and above all by his disharmony, that is to say: the co-existence in him of certain highly developed abilities with an atrophy of others, so that he will show, now too much, now too little, temperament, ambition, urge for self-assertion, and capacity for love. We find in him a sociologically reduced capacity for adaptation; a lack of ability to shape his own line of conduct, to create his own framework of values. In short, his innate quality of being different is either a sickly mental disposition, with a tendency toward a psychosis, or else he is an unfavorably abnormal variant of the species homo sapiens: in any case, as far as the vital functions are concerned he is —in some fashion or other—negative. "Psychopathy implies: to become unfit for the breeding of offspring. It would be inhuman to try to cross members of talented families with a heterogeneous strain. To be even remotely pre-destined for the fate of genius means, most of the time and as a rule, to be doomed to a gruesome martyrdom." According to Bleuler, psychopathy signifies an inferiority of certain defined tendencies, which inferiority may be passed on to the progeny and is liable to diminish the potential for adaptation.

In Kraepelin's opinion, psychopathy is "a deviation from mental health, in the sense of degeneration and inferiority, and a permanent modification of the life work

106

through a dispositional deficiency in the fields of emotion and will-power, simultaneous with a lack of constancy in the development of the personality."

For Tunksfeld,[32] the psychopath is a human being that suffers from its abnormal mental attributes and, in turn, makes mankind suffer from them.

In the view of Kauders,[33] the most striking feature is the disproportion among the various psychic factors.

If, instead of viewing as a whole the syndrome characteristic for the psychopath of genius disposition, we turn to its single component elements, namely: inattention, craving for solitude, absorption, distraction, irritability, spite, obstinacy, unpredictability, urge for self-assertion, lack of will-power, insufficient adaptability, and disharmony, consisting in an over-development of certain abilities with the simultaneous atrophy of other qualities, we are afforded a deeper insight into these obscure interrelations. It is an undeniable and undenied experience that the entire complex of the above attributes is never found in one and the same individual. We obtain at once a wholly new concept of the relations of these attributes to each other, and to the psychopathy of genius, when—rather than inquire into the origins of that psychopathy—we investigate its single elements.

The psychopath of genius disposition appears weak of will only whenever he does not choose to "will." In all acts pointed toward the goal of his "willing" he exerts the strength of an athlete, he manifests a will-power that does not tolerate any diversion. The most intense concentration is an indispensable prerequisite for the accomplishment of extraordinary achievements. The outer aspect of this particular situation is, quite naturally, that of a monomania accompanied by absent-mindedness, a craving for solitude, etc. This craving, for instance, may express itself in a philosopher's or an artist's forsaking the big city for a remote, solitary place far from the maddening crowd, in a scientist's shutting himself up in

107

his laboratory. A man of wit, like Disraeli, was often in-midst of many people so engrossed in his own thoughts that no one dared approach him.

The connections which we are discussing will be yet more sharply clarified by the following utterances, which are significant expressions of the feelings and thoughts of those that delivered them. Byron once said: "Society is harmful to any achievement of the mind." We may also quote these words of Goethe, who often fled to Jena, because he found solitude there: "Nothing will change the fact that I cannot produce the least thing without absolute loneliness. Once again I made the experience that I can work only in absolute solitude, and that, not only conversation, but even the very presence in my house of loved and esteemed persons at once diverts my poetic sources. I feel that my nature craves but composure and a favorable mood, and will not enjoy anything that hampers those." Wagner: "A master needs quiet. Calm and quiet are his most imperative needs. Isolation and complete loneliness are my only consolation, and my salvation." Johannes Mueller, the physiologist, said:[34] "The only consolations for the lack of sympathetic friends, which I feel deeply, are my home, my work, my solitude!"

Furthermore, closer examination will show that the elements subsumed under the term "psychopathy" are of different origin, that what is called psychopathy is not invariably pathological, nor is it congenital: it is much rather acquired in the course of life. Viewed from this angle, it reveals itself as the physiological correlate to an extraordinary claim made on the powers of an individual by an overwhelmingly great task. That the presumably most conspicuous single attribute of the psychopath of genius disposition—his disharmony—must not be inter-preted as a pathological feature, can be shown most clearly by pointing to the parallels apparent in the realm of physiology. Whether in a social community, an

108

individual, an organ, or even in as small a unit as a cell, whenever a craving induced by environmental peculiarities reaches a degree of intensity that the desire for satisfaction compels the individual to work to exhaustion, all other activities will soon be reduced to a minimum: any particular intensity of one single capacity always appears combined with a diminution or the suppression of all other capacities, or functions. As soon as a glandular cell proceeds to divide, it ceases secreting. This is true also of cells that form a glandular carcinoma: as soon as the growth of the latter lays claim to all the cell's energies, the previous secretion activity is terminated. Because of its specialization for the specific function which it has to perform as a component part of the nervous system, the ganglion cell loses the ability, found in other cells, to switch over to lower function if and when the need arises.

Whenever a danger threatens life and thus brings into play all forces in an effort to obviate that danger, all other activities will be suppressed . . . Whenever an organ is fixed upon one specific task, it loses its ability to substitute for the functions of other organs. When we want to hear precisely, we close our eyes; when a person wants to measure a distance with his eyes, he avoids any diversion by sounds. When a man, wrapped in thought, turns his senses toward his inner voices he does neither hear nor see what passes around him: his outer senses are silenced. An immoderate imagination impedes reasonable judgment, just as much as the latter prevents an over-abundance of imagination . . . The heat of passion makes us forget our finest principles.

Recognition of the fact that any effort driven to the utmost of a man's capacity automatically restricts his capacities in other fields permits us to understand a whole series of experiences which, until now, had seemed incoherent; the fact, for instance, that great teachers are often bad scientists, good musicians bad composers, and

109

that a philosopher may be a weakling, an athlete mentally underprivileged.

In this connection we must also mention cases of almost complete idiocy combined with a one-sided talent for music, painting, or mathematics. We can furthermore refer to certain defects observed in child prodigies, as the case of a little violinist who, contrary to his contemporaries, proved unable to bend a piece of wire into the simplest geometric form, or the case of an eight year old boy, who was an outstanding chess player, and yet had no awareness whatever of the flora and fauna in which he lived, was unable to register any dates, and could not recognize even a simple coin.

Also noteworthy are certain declarations by famous artists and scientists. Byron, for instance, found the pictures of Velasquez or Murillo "unbearably boring." To Darwin Shakespeare was so tedious that he caused him nausea. "My taste for paintings and music" (he once wrote) "I also lost almost entirely. Yet books on history, biographies, and travel reports interest me as vividly as ever." Richard Wagner explained in a letter to Mathilde Wesendonk: "When I find myself in this state of inner unrest, no picture, no piece of plastic art has any effect on me. Nothing that has but 'local' importance, even though it be a great masterpiece, gives me any entertainment, I remain indifferent to all these things; in truth, I am dead to everything that is outside me, I see nothing but my inner visions, and they are crying out for sound, nothing but sound. All I am striving for is to be allowed to follow my inner creative urge, which is as lively as ever . . . There must be in us a certain, indescribable, sense that reaches a maximum of activity and clarity only when those senses which are turned outward are but dreaming: whenever I do not really see and hear accurately, that sense is at its most active and manifests its function as productive unrest."

This necessity to gather all one's powers for the solution of one single task explains furthermore the surprising fact that, as a rule, geniuses share most of the prejudices of their time and often do not even see that the latter are in contradiction to the new concepts they have created. Kepler, whose aunt had still been burned as a witch, believed that witchcraft was an undeniable fact. Newton searched for an explanation of the Apocalypse. Guericke, the inventor of the pneumatic pump, concerned himself with such problems as where heaven, hell, and the last judgment were located. . . . Besides clear physical ideas, the mathematician Euler dealt in his books with such questions as whether the devil could work miracles. . . . Pascal believed in miracles; Tycho assumed the earth to be in the center of the world.

Yet even those whose mental powers are not all absorbed in the struggle for one great task often show only very little comprehension for the progress of their times; history supplies us with many such examples. Long after its publication, the book of Copernicus was made a laughingstock by comedians; Kepler's teachings were called blasphemous figments of the brain by certain theologians. Newton's great discovery found a more general acceptance only 27 years after it had been formulated, thanks to Voltaire's pointing to its significance. It took decades for the ideas of Lamarck and Gregor Mendel, for the experiments of Lavoisier, for the works of Laplace, for Auenbrugger's, the Vienna physician's, new method of lung examination, to be appreciated according to their merits. Jenner's vaccination against smallpox was branded as the devil's own invention, and he was made the topic of many a caricature. For Roentgen's discovery a very restricted field of usefulness was predicted, and in 1900 it was prophesied that the airplane would have no future as a passenger-carrying vehicle. Even the experiments on radioactivity by Becquerel, which opened a new epoch in practical natural science, created a sensation only after radioactive substances had been discovered whose radioactivity was several million times superior to that of uranium.

2

GENIUS AND PSYCHOSIS

It is easy to see why the simultaneous occurrence of genius and genuine insanity should have given food for serious reflection. Whenever the insanity, be it that of a philosopher or of a man of religion, transferred its effects to the realm of social life or gained influence upon the march of history, a thorough exploration of that phenomenon was indicated. The same was true when in the paintings of an artist like Van Gogh the mentally abnormal reached a striking degree. Particularly amazing was, of course, the observation that in a small number of cases, as evidenced in the biographies of famous as well as of obscure inmates of lunatic asylums, extraordinary mental abilities were present in the course of a grave illness of the mind. In some of these cases an already pre-existing talent may have emerged more clearly owing to the disappearance of normally existing inhibitions, whereby certain hidden aspects of the personality involved were enabled to manifest themselves.

In such men as the Swiss novelist Conrad F. Meyer and the Austrian composer Hugo Wolff the mania phases of their disease regularly called forth a truly feverish urge for production. Nietzsche, Hölderlin, Van Gogh, Maupassant, Kleist not only derived from their dreamlike ecstatic condition an intensification of their achievements, they also (or at least some of them) reached the highest summits of their artistic creation shortly before their final destruction, and in a number of them we observe a change in style at this same juncture. Dostoievsky quite consciously utilized the periods of premonition

112

(aura) preceding his epileptic fits to describe mentally abnormal types: "In this condition I write much more and much better than usual. Formerly, whenever I found myself in such a nervous condition, I used it for writing." [35]

More recent investigations have not supported Lombroso's assumption that a mental disease can make an ungifted person gifted, or that a head injury as well as degeneration or idiocy can induce the quality of genius. Many of the pictures painted by mentally ill persons were produced at the doctor's suggestion, and very few of them were attempted without any previous training. "The growing recognition of the importance of art in occupational therapy has led at present to the concept that the spontaneous productions of the insane were an attempt at self-healing. The patient tries to express his inner torment in art to find a release by objectifying his emotions in a poem or a picture." [36] "The feelings of a secret guilt uproots the very foundations of the psyche of those who are victims of this so-called 'compensatory illness.'" [37]

We can perhaps contribute to the comprehension of the coincidence of insanity and genius by pointing to the fact that a high degree of emotional upheaval is an essential causative factor in either condition. It is doubtful that there ever exists a state of complete calm in our consciousness. There is reason to assume (as Jung does) that even the simplest conscious sensation is, though possibly only in traces, "affect-accented," that is: accompanied by emotion. When our blood reaches a state of ebullience where the need for the relaxation of the prevalent mental tensions arises, efforts set in to re-establish an equilibrium. The manner in which the various component parts of our consciousness associate with each other to form thoughts, actions, etc., determines whether one man sees things more clearly than another, whether he produces spiritual values, or becomes mentally infer-

113

ior, ill, and so on. In any case, this collaboration of the two groups of forces deriving from hereditary disposition and environment must suffice us for an explanation of the multiplicity of the forms in which the mind expresses itself: there are no other impelling powers to set our mind in motion.

As some psychoanalysts have assumed, dreams can secure undisturbed sleep by causing the illusion of wish-fulfillment. Many illusions have obviously a similar purpose: to reassure. When emotional excitability reaches an extraordinary degreee of intensity—occasionally in healthy people, but much more frequently in mentally ill persons—it may express itself in daydreams, that is, in hallucinations. Those sentenced to death dream of innocence and liberation. Thus Gretchen in Goethe's "Faust";

Ich bin nun ganz in deiner Macht
Lass mich zuerst das Kind noch tränken
Sie nahmen mirs um mich zu kränken
und sagen nun ich hätt' es umgebracht.

(I am all yours because you willed it
Yet first to nurse my child you must reprieve me
They took it from me to aggrieve me
And now they say 'twas I who killed it.)

In an acute state of starvation, even a modern educated man may have hallucinations: he suddenly believes to see baskets full of the most splendid fruits, platters heaped with the juiciest roasts. The visions St. Jerome saw during his fast can also be explained in this manner, as can be the custom observed in some Indian tribes which orders the one destined to conjure the spirits in order to consult with them before setting out on a serious enterprise, to withdraw into solitude for a several days' fast.

Chapter IV

1

THE THEORY OF ASSOCIATION AND THE GESTALT THEORY

All these mental images—dreams, illusions, hallucinations—are products of the imagination, that is to say: combinations of memories and conceptions present in our consciousness, either with each other or with new perceptions.

The association of elements of our consciousness caused by the collaboration of the ganglion cells of the nervous system can also assume different forms. Not only imagination, but intellect, character, will, are also the products of associations. So are our qualities and attributes, which are by no means ultimate units.

Qualities such as "good" and "bad" our imagination is able to transpose into the notions of witches, sorcerers, gods, devils, into concepts like heaven and hell, of a supra-sensorial and subterranean world. Associational components are furthermore the source of fairy tales, fables, myths, legends, of superstition, mysticism, and occultism. Yet the finest blossoms of the human mind stem from the same source: religion, art, science.

Once we assume this interplay of elementary forces deriving from hereditary disposition and environment, it is not difficult to understand that their association appears now under the aspect of health now under the aspect of mental illness; now in the form of a great accomplishment, now in the guise of a neurosis, a phobia, melancholy, hysteria, claustrophibia, and even insanity. We then also understand how a circumstance harmful to life may favor the origin of a genius achievement. We understand how bad qualities, such as egoism, contrariness, pride, frigidity of temperament, prejudices, under-estimation of difficulties (in an enterprise that without such under-estimation might never have been undertaken) can be instrumental in the achievement of a favorable purpose. We understand, finally, that even insanity may contribute to the accomplishments of genius, and still more to the fame of genius, when obstinacy is taken for heroism, and vagueness for originality.

The much observed inter-relation between genius and insanity requires a separate investigation. The "one-sidedness" and the mono-maniac quality with which the genius pursues his object, and the idee fixe of the madman on the other hand can easily induce confused concepts, especially when the genius also produces hallucinations, a symptom frequently observed in the insane, or when the madman comes up with the inspirations of a genius. What distinguishes them decisively and fundamentally, is the success of their efforts. The spasmodic endeavors of the insane to restore a mental equilibrium lead him, uneconomical and fruitless as they are, always deeper into the system of his madness so that, in the end, no exit is left open to him. The genius, on the other hand, accomplishes the solution of his chosen task in a fashion so far superior to that of those who tried their hand at it before him that he becomes the object of general admiration.

The contrast between the senseless behavior of the insane and the highly meaningful comportment of the genius is tersely formulated in a statement by Kretsch-

116

mer: "There are successful and unsuccessful inventors; the unsuccessful ones are called paranoics."

The theory of association, to which we have referred, is however not generally accepted. Even among those that admit its usefulness doubts are voiced whether that theory is applicable to all physiological occurrences, and to all mental formations. "This question of principle: whether all formations originate by way of association, or else whether there also exists such a phenomenon as "free-rising" formations, cannot be answered." (Jaspers.)

Many authors rather agree with the following assumption: "performances as complex as our perceptions and single-purposed actions are not simple summations or additive figures of sensations, composed of separate elementary sensations" (Encyclopedia Britannica). This theory asserts that we never experience single impressions, but rather and exclusively "structures," "Gestalten," which—corresponding to each new experience—are immediately set off against a diffuse, neutral field as a new entity. Such a Gestalt as is, for instance, produced by the transposition of a melody into another key cannot be accounted for (so this theory says) by the simple addition of separate sensations; it can be explained only by the assumption of a particular form of cognition, based on an extraordinary disposition. A melody (the partisans of this argument continue) does not represent a mere mechanical serialization; its notes appear in harmonic order. The entity, although its parts remain distinguishable, is invariably more than the sum of those parts. Intuitively perceived Gestalten have a necessarily closed structure (Burgkamp), and frequently very concrete attributes, dominated by intrinsic laws and characterized by the tendency toward entity, while their parts are conditioned by that entity. (see Werthheimer, W. Koehler, Ehrenfels.)

However, the origin of a "flash of thought," which all of a sudden clarifies obscure connections for the scientist endowed with the discipline of thinking, cannot be explained satisfactorily by this theory of Gestalt. The emergence of an intuition becomes explicable when we refer to the experience that such intuition usually has its point of departure in a detail that attracts particular attention within a given field of investigation; the observation of that detail is then followed by a long series of releases. Most of these associations remain below the boundary of consciousness, and often enough only the initial and the final link become conscious. "A fortuitous chain of circumstances" participates in the production of intuition. In an effort to underline the fact that the point of departure of the intuition remains obscure, Bechterev opposes the latter, under the term "independent association," to associations released immediately by external impressions.

The practical criterion of value will serve to answer the question which of these two theories is to be preferred; after all, it is the purpose of any theory to be useful within the practice of life.

The following judgments by two well-known authors will contribute to a correct evaluation of the two contrasting theories. "The mechanistic explanation must always remain the methodological ideal of all cognition, even where it has so far been impossible—and may forever remain impossible—to reveal that mechanism completely." (Vaihinger). "A biological entity has never yet produced one single biological truth, whereas quite frequently a scientist has succeeded in revealing the principle of organic composition by putting together stones obtained through specialized investigation." (M. Hartmann.)

In order to formulate an opinion of our own, we must above all take into account the various objections that have been raised against the theory of association. Here they are: there is an unsurmountable borderline between body and soul; while a parallelism exists, there is no interaction; both are eternally separated from each other.

In fact, however, the two together form the human organism, and interaction between the physical and the psychic is easy to prove. Latent energies of the body may appear in the realm of the mind, while mental energies can become submerged in the physical substance; confidence, hope, or joy can stimulate the weary senses; a situation calling for responsible action may sober up a man who is intoxicated; courage and awareness of strength heighten resistance to infection, while anxieties and worries lower it; pulse, respiration, blood pressure, and secretion can be influenced by mental factors: in a fit of anger the biliary flow is suspended. Many organic diseases are of mental origin, even grave disturbances in the circulation system, in the gastro-intestinal tract (stomach ulcers, for instance), in the liver or the bile duct, in the sex organs, in metabolism; or diseases like a rash, blister formation, skin hemorrhages, asthma, exophthalmic goiter, and so on. Excitement may be the cause of gastric catarrh and jaundice. Thus not only nervous conditions, that is to say dynamic changes, but even genuine organic illnesses, accompanied by a change of anatomic structure, can be produced by mental factors. The existence of a regular dependence between digestion and mental functions was demonstrated experimentally by Pavlov, for instance when he increased metabolism by a suggested sensation of cold. By connecting a human being into a sensitive galvanic circuit we can show the influence of emotions, as they are registered in the oscillations of the current.[38]

On the other hand, the influence of the body on the mind can also be observed. Grave fatigue turns even the most differentiated creature of culture into a primitive. Uncontrolled sexual stimuli, as well as an unrelieved bladder or rectum, may release dream pictures at the same time as mental tensions. Acquired blindness or deafness can change not only the facial expression and

119

the physical posture but the mental attitude of a person. Primitive impulses, such as the sex impulse, may manifest themselves not only in an affect but also in ethical acts.[39]

A second objection asserts that matters of mind cannot be measured like matters physical. There is (so this objection maintains) no measuring unit for ethical phenomena. It is true that similar units as meter, gram, atom, molecule, which all represent accepted values, cannot be produced for the field of ethics; the reason for this, however, lies in the fact that mental and physical data merge into each other without any sharp line of demarcation so that it is impossible for anybody to say where the one ends and the other begins. If, as we have demonstrated, there is interaction between body and mind, then there must be transitional zones between sensations that are to be interpreted as "mental," that is to say conscious, and emotions that remain unconscious or subconscious. If, as experience shows, even the simplest conscious sensation contains an affective component (a conclusion also drawn by Jung, in his "Energetics of the Mind"), if sensation represents a collective of yet simpler sensations, then the measuring unit suitable for both mental and physical data cannot be but one and the same: an energy unit.

The very fact that mental and physical phenomena merge into each other suggests the assumption that in the realm of the mental, too, no other laws can have validity than the laws of nature, which have been established for the realm of the physical. The "law of energy" —presumably the most comprehensive among those laws known so far—appears particularly suited to illustrate the soundness of our assertion.

All the various partial processes that compose the act of thinking turn out to be, when viewed under the angle of energy, tools the use of which contributes in some fashion to the grand total of energy required for the attainment of a set goal, be it that they directly increase that sum, be it that by preventing a diminution of effectiveness they save energy. The act of observing as well as the gathering of observations means an increase in energy. Bringing order into these observations will show where we have collected a sufficient quantity, and where gaps in our experience remain to be filled. This facilitates comparisons, the revelation of similarities and divergencies, and thus permits us to perceive (with a reduced expenditure of attention) analogies which, in turn, make possible the transfer of previous experiences to a new field. Measuring helps in the clarification of concepts where the senses are not acute enough for the task. Making notes, since it relieves our memory, assists in joining the elements of consciousness most fitted to each other. Analysis helps to avoid a waste of strength by drawing attention to the essential points. Words, notes, chemical formulae, geometrical drawings, and other symbols derived from past experience facilitate the development of the mind towards higher aims, by allowing us to operate with "abstract" notions.

Long ago, Ernst Mach pointed to the economic significance of algebraic operations for the purposes of scientific exploration: "By using addition, multiplication, logarithms, and other mathematical operations, we relieve our heads, and make unnecessary the repetition of calculations already made. In the equation

$$\frac{x^2-y^2}{x+y} = x-y$$

whatever the actual figures for x and y may be, the complex figures on the left always appear replaced by simpler ones on the right. In mathematical operations any brain work at all may be dispensed with by symbolizing counting operations carried out many centuries ago with the signs of mechanical operations, and by thus saving the functions of the brain, instead of wasting them on algebra operations previously performed, for important

121

cases, similarly to what a merchant does who, instead of pushing his boxes and cases himself, proceeds by ordering them pushed."

A geometrical figure has a similar function. Anybody familiar with the theorem of Pythagoras can see at one glance that, in a right-angled triangle, the square of the hypotenuse equals the sum of the squares over the sides.

In the same fashion, every theory enables us to husband our strength. It puts in the place of innumerable experiences a general judgment as a symbol and, by offering a precise, ordered collection of experiences, it saves us a lot of separate observations, descriptions, and controls. Being a simple, precise instruction for imitative repetition, it makes it possible for us to replace things that are difficult of conception, because they are unusual, by notions easy to grasp, because usual, and it thereby permits the solution of many tasks that are difficult and might otherwise remain insoluble. The conquest of new cognitions, which often remain out of reach for the practical man despite all his great efforts, frequently becomes child's play for the scientist familiar with the theory. "As soon as the law of refraction became known, it became unnecessary to determine singly every case of refraction for the various material combinations and angles of incidence. Instead of determining innumerable such cases for these various material combinations and angles of incidence, all we have to remember is the formula

$$\frac{\text{Sin a}}{\text{Sin b}} = n$$

and the values for "n," which is much easier. . . . The mechanism of all the necessary calculations has been established, once and for all, in the analytical mechanics of Lagrange. Whatever slight thought process the individual case may still require can be supplied by mechanic brain work."[40]

122

In the handling of machines, too, theoretical knowledge has an economizing effect. If one knows the principle that guides the functioning of the machine, there is no need to attend to any details.

The history of medicine also offers many examples how an advance in knowledge and technique permits savings in effort: the concepts that led to the protective vaccination against smallpox, now generally practiced, were still most complicated; the procedure as handled today has all the smoothness of a mechanical operation.

It is the meaning and the purpose of every "urge for knowledge," of all striving for technical perfection, to make adaptation easier.

Our improved knowledge of the nature of diseases enables today every beginner to diagnose many illnesses without much wracking of the brain, with more speed and greater certainty than were formerly at the disposal of the most experienced physician. . . . The saving of work which an act of intuition, obtained with seeming ease, or technical improvements makes possible by rendering superfluous all further search for new hypotheses and by simplifying the process of adaptation, can be assumed to be one of the reasons for the high esteem in which they are held. In some manner, all the various apparatuses, tools, and methods which man keeps on inventing incessantly, and also the manifold goods offered for sale serve that same purpose of saving strength. This holds true also of the means which, up to now, has served greatly to simplify the exchange of goods: money. All efforts tend towards a reduction in the consumption of strength, toward an easier, cheaper, improved, and more complete satisfaction of all needs. No detail work expended in the process of thinking appears superfluous: all of it contributes somehow or other to an economical satisfaction of needs.

All experience has shown again and again that work is the determining moment. The mind needs energy as urgently as a machine does fuel. Even the most decayed idea preserves itself as long as no energy is spent on destroying it.

An effort once made retains some kind of value for all times, and it is of no consequence whether that effort was made by one individual or by many, or even by generations, whether it took a short while or a long time, nor does it matter in what sequence the work proceeded, if only any possible deficit on the one side of the ledger was made up for by a plus sign on the other.

2

FINAL RÉSUMÉ

The following is a summary of the assumptions and conclusions which I have derived from the above investigations: these assumptions and conclusions differ essentially from those of other investigators of the problem of genius.

The capacity for inspiration and for any accomplishment of genius dimensions is not the remote effect of a hereditary disposition. Experience and knowledge, environmental products both, are of no less significance for the formation of our mind than original disposition, and as concerns the differences of intelligence in different individuals, experience and knowledge are of greater importance than membership in a certain race.

Nor is the achievement of genius the consequence of a pathologically abnormal mental condition; as numerous parallels in the field of physiology suggest, it remains rather within the realm of the normal. Once this complex of symptoms that goes by the name of "psychopathy of genius" is dissolved into its component elements, we see (and this insight carries almost the conviction of experimental proof) why it is that evil experiences, serious reverses, bad original qualities, and even a mental disease may occasionally further genius as much as an extraordinary disposition. The only thing that matters is that they must also create a spur to increased effort.

The determining factor is, exclusively, the effort invested in the attainment of a set goal, that is to say: the grand total of energies, the component terms of which sum are the forces of hereditary disposition, of environment, and of individual effort. That this role of the individual effort is obvious to any objective observation may be seen from the following opinion of the Spanish physiologist Ramon y Cajal: "Every great work is the fruit of patience, perseverance, and concentration—during months and years—upon one specific subject. He who wants to discover a new truth must be capable of the strictest abstinence and renunciation. The ideal case would be that of a scientist who, during this period of mental incubation, would pay no heed to any thought that is extraneous to his problem, like the somnambulist who listens only to the words of the hypnotizer. If he possesses this capacity to remain incessantly absorbed by one subject, he will be able to multiply his strength. . . . When we ponder over this strange attribute of man which enables him to heighten his mental powers by letting himself be absorbed by a subject or a problem, we are compelled to arrive at the conception that the brain, on the grounds of its retentive faculty and owing to a continual adaptation to a given task, is capable of further anatomical and dynamic development." [41]

Thus, to become a genius is by no means to be doomed by fate, nor does the psychopathy of genius constitute a danger for progeny.

While it is true that need often acts as a motor that sets in motion great powers, it is nevertheless a fact that optimum conditions for successful creation and surprising achievements are closely connected with the "pleasure accent" that accompanies the effort itself. If Goethe, perhaps one of the happiest geniuses ever, has said: "you may rest assured that I was not happy. Not even for four weeks, if you want to add up all the shining hours of my life. It was like the eternal rolling of a rock that wanted to be lifted again and again. Too many were the claims that were made on my activities, from the outside as well as within me . . .", we do not have to take this too literally: after all, these are the words of the man who called personality "the supreme happiness of the sons of this earth."

Even intellectuals such as Mill, Nietzsche, Spencer, who were afflicted by long stretches of grave physical illness, have confessed that they would not have wanted to exchange their ways of life with any other.

Kretschmer once formulated the theoretically correct concept that inbreeding, over many generations, within talented families—possibly by crossing a talent disposition with slightly different blood, or coupling similar hereditary substances of superior values—might produce a greater number of individuals of high value. This theory, however, has for a long time to come so slim a chance of being put into practice that the desired increase in the number of genius accomplishments might be obtained earlier if, instead of waiting until we have learned how to couple fittingly genes of superior value, we rather try to learn how to exploit, more methodically than heretofore, our environment for the attainment of our purposes. Creative achievements make such enormous claims upon the working power of the individual that any waste of that power on work that is easily obtainable from other sources would constitute a danger to the achievements of the individual. It is quite unnecessary that we should hew every stone with our own hands, or carve the beam we need ourselves; in short:

126

that we should insist on producing everything out of our own resources; nor is there any need for us to sit and wait, inactively, until an unexpected lucky coincidence presents us with a fruitful thought. Indeed, we can—by our conscious efforts—prepare its appearance.

NOTES

THE ORIGIN OF REASON

1 *See* "Heterotype Hypothesis," Garret Harding, *Scientific Monthly,* March 1950.

2 Alexis Carrel: *Man the Unknown*, N.Y., Harper, 1935.

3 Rittenberg, cited by v. Bartalanffy, Ottawa Univ. Sc. January 13, 1950. "The Theory of Open Systems in Physics and Biology."

4 Quoted from Leonard Thomas Troland by Jerome Alexander, "Life, Its Nature and Origin" *Scientific Monthly*, Aug., 1949.

5 Deficiency of A—night blindness
             "   " B—beriberi, polyneuritis
             "   " C—scurvy
             "   " D—rickets
             "   " E—inability of female to carry fetus to term
             "   " K—severe hemorrhages due to reduced coagulability of the blood

6 Harvey Cushing: "A Biography" by John Fulton, Springfield, Ill. Ch. C. Thomas, 1946, pp. 299, 300.

7 Burr: "Field Theory in Biology."
See "Pasteur," Biography by R. Jules Dubos, Little, Brown, 1950.

9 Benjamin Harrow, *Scientific Monthly*, March 1947.

10 Fr. H. Johnsen: "Heat and Life," *Amer. Science*, September 1954.

11 *See* "Heterotype Hypothesis," Garret Harding, *Scientific Monthly*, March 1950.

12 Waldemar Kaempfert.

13 Recently scientists succeeded not only in crystallizing other plant viruses but also the virus of the disease polio. See *The New York Times*, November 6, 1955.

14 Pottenger, F .M.: "Symptoms of Visceral Diseases," 6th ed. St. Louis, The Mosby Co., 1944.

15 Arndt-Schulz.

16 If external factors supporting the perpetuation of life act regu-

larly and continuously, then we do not speak of stimuli, but of conditions of life. Such life processes are called "automatic."

17 Meisenheimer: *"Geschlecht und Geschlechter"* (Sex and Genders).

18 Encyclopedia Britannica.

19 V. Bartalanffy, *see* his "Theory of Open Systems."

20 *See* Nägeli and the Psycholamarckists.

21 Pavlov.

22 Bleuler: *"Geschichte der Seele und ihres Bewusstseins"* (History of the Soul and Its Consciousness). Berlin, Springer, 1932;—*"Der Autismus in der Medizin"* (Autism in Medicine). Münch. Med. Wochenschrift 1931, H. 19.

23 Economo: *"Probleme der Hirnforschung"* (Problems of Brain Investigation).

24 Ramon y Cajal, *see: "Regeln und Ratschläge"* (Rules and Counsels), verl. Reinhardt, München.

25 Julian Huxley: "Darwinism Today: On Living in a Revolution." Harper, New York, London.

26 De Vries.

27 G. G. Simpson: "Meaning of Evolution," New Haven, Yale University Press, 1949.

28 *See* "Life, Its Nature and Origin," Jerome Alexander, *Scientific Monthly*, August 1948 and S. J. Holmes: "What is Natural Selection?" *Scientific Monthly*, November 1948.

29 Simpson.

30 *See* A. Hock: "The Origin of Genius."

31 H. S. Jennings: "Behavior of the Lower Organisms," 1906.

32 Fechner.

33 A. Hoche: *"Vom Sinne des Schmerzes"* (On the Meaning of Pain). F. Lehmann, München.

34 Karl Bühler.

35 Mosso.

36 Bechterev: "Reflex-psychology."

37 Both kinds of reactions—instincts as well as reflexes—are preformed; the former, however, concern the whole creature.

38 "Great Experiments in Psychology," H. E. Garret, D. Appleton, Century Co., New York. London.
Century Co., New York, London; and "Animal Psychology," Frank A. Beach, *Nat. Hist.* October 1947.

39 Pfungst.

40 Robert M. Yerkes: "Chimpanzees, a Laboratory Colony." Yale University Press, 1943.

41 "Animal Psychology," Frank A. Beach, *Nat. Hist.* October 1947.

42 E. Pokolsky: "The Genius and the Brain," *Med. Rec.* March 1946.

43 Grosser, Med. Klin. 1931, p. 43.

44 Ramon y Cajal.

45 O. Poetzel and L. Horn, Wien. Klin. Woch. 1933, H. 44.

46 Riese: "*Gehirn des Linkshänders*" (Brain of Left-handed Persons). Deutsch. Med. Woch. 1938, H. 26.

47 Economo: "*Beobachtungen bei Encephalitis lethargica*" (Observations on Encephalitis Lethargice).

48 Waldemar Kaempfert, *The New York Times*, February 4, 1951.

49 Dr. P. B. Porter and A. C. Griffin, Stanford, Dr. King.

50 Levy-Brühl: "*Die Seele des Primitiven*" (The Soul of Primitive Man). Wien, 1930.

51 Sigmund Freud.

52 Jakob Burckhardt: "*Griechische Kulturgeschichte*" (History of Greek Culture).

53 S. A. Hoche.

54 Grosser, Deutsch. Med. Woch. 1938, H. 1.

55 S. A. Hoche: "*Vom Sinne des Schmerzes*" (On the Meaning of Pain). Verl. F. L. Lehmann, München.

56 Pfungst: "*Die Bedeutung der Affenbiologie für die Menschen*" (The Importance of the Biology of Apes to Man). Berlin. Med. Gesellsch. 1942; and Dexler: "*Verhandlungen des Lotos*" (Transactions of the "Lotus"). Prag.

57 Encyclopedica Britannica under: Psychology, comparative.

58 Katz: "*Aufbau der Tastwelt*" (Growth of the World of Touch). Münch. Med. Woch. 1925, H. 50.

59 1939 by Funk & Wagnals Co., New York—London.

60 Goethe: "*Iphigenie auf Tauris.*"

61 The words of a child become clearer and its speech more precise. It actually speaks only when it begins not merely to imitate vowels, but also gains control of its vocal muscles. It speaks to the degree that this control is gained.

62 Egyptian writing is some centuries younger than Sumerian writing in Mesopotamia and developed under the stimulus of the Mesopotamian civilization.

63 *See* Rappoport: "History of Hieroglyph," Vol. III, London.

64 Friedrich Nietzsche.

65 *See* "Review of *The Earth as a Planet*," by Lloyd V. Berker, University of Chicago Press, *Sc. Am.* September 1955.

NOTES

THE ORIGIN OF GENIUS

1 Alfred Hock: *"Die methodische Entwicklung der Talente und des Genies"* (The methodical development of talent and genius). Leipzig, Akademische Verlagsgesellschaft.

2 "A great man: one who affects the mind of his generation." (Disraeli)

3 Ernst Kretschmer: *"Erbbiologische Bedingtheiten"* (Conditions of Biological Inheritance). Med. Klin. 1934, H. 7 . . . *"Das Genie."* Verlag Enke . . . *"Familiäre und stammesmässige Zuechtungsformen bei Psychosen"* (Family and Tribal Breeding Forms in Psychoses). Münch. Med. Woch. 1930, H. 35 . . . *"Der Aufbau der Persönlichkeit"* (The Growth of Personality). Klin. Woch. 1935, H. 2.

4 Carrel: *"Man, the Unknown."*

5 Rahmer, in Lange-Eichbaum. Springer. Berlin. 1931.

6 Hugo Iltis. Wien. Klin. Woch. October 1924.

7 Part of this last quotation is a retranslation into English from a German translation. (Translator's note)

8 Strumpel: *"Über Erbanlage und Verbrechen* (On Hereditary Disposition and Crime). Klin. Woch. 1935, H. 11.

9 Joh. Lange: *"Psychiatrische Fragen für den praktischen Arzt"* (Psychiatric Questions for the General Practitioner). Münch. Med. Woch. 1930, H. 97.—Münch. Med. Woch. 1929, H. 22—Same, 1932, H. 42.

10 *See*: Hock, loc. cit.

11 *See*: Biography of Humboldt by Helmut de Terra, p. 248.

12 W. Martin: *"Altholländische Bilder"* (Old Dutch Paintings).

13 J. Burckhardt.

14 Georg Brandes: *"Geschichte der Literatur des 19 Jahrhunderts"* (History of 19th Century Literature).

15 Brandes: loc. cit.

16 Josef Hofmiller. Neue Deutsche Rundschau. 1920.

17 James Israel: *"Nierenblutungen aus dunkler Ursache"* (Kidney Bleeding from Obscure Causes).

18 Bahle. 15th German Congress of Psychologists. 1936.

19 In Oscar Levant: *"My Life."* Doubleday, Doran. 1940, p. 160.

20 Letter of 1498.

21 *See* H. Hadviger, Basel: *"Tierdressur als wissenschaftliche Methode"* (The Taming of Animals as a Scientific Method). *Also*: Dexler: *"Die Lehre von dem Gestalten als Grundlage der Tierpsychologie"* (The Teaching of *Gestalten* as Basis of Animal Psychology). Lotos. Prague. 1923.

22 Boswell: *"The Life of Dr. Johnson."*

23 M. F. Ashley Montague: *"Vesalius and the Glenists,"* Scientific Monthly, April 1955.

24 D. S. Mirsky: *"Lenin."* Ed. by O. Burdett. The Holm Press.

25 Ernest J. Simmons: *"Leo Tolstoy."* Little, Brown.

26 E. A. Poe, Pocketbook Edition.

27 Hansemann: *"Das Gehirn von Hermann v. Helmholtz"* (The Brain of Hermann Von Helmholtz). Barth, Leipz. 1908.

28 Alphonse Much.

29 *See* loc. cit.

30 *"Werden und Wesen der Geistesarbeit"* (Development and Nature of Intellectual Work). Deutsch. Med. Woch. 1933.

31 Luxemburger: *"Erblichkeit, Eugenik, Bevölkerungspolitik"* (Heredity. Eugenics and Population Policy). Münch. Med. L. 1930.

32 Tunksfeld: *"Zur Beurteilung psychopathischer Persönlichkeiten"* (On Judging Psychopathic Personalities). Med. Kl. 1930/25.

33 *"Psychopathie und Psychose als Grenzgebiete der Nervenheilkunde"* (Psychopathy and Psychosis as Border Areas of Nerve Therapy). Wiener Med. Woch. 1936/H. 20. . . . *"Einführung des werdenden Arztes in die Seelenheilkunde"* (Introduction to Spiritual Therapy for the Novice Physician). Wien. Kl. Woch. 1937. Scharf: *"Geniales Trinkertum"* (Alcoholism of Genius). D. Med. Woch. 1938. H. 34. Storch: *"Krankheit und schöpferische Leistung"* (Disease and Creative Work). Münch. Med Woch, 1925. Schroeder: *"Psychopathie und abnorme Characktere"* (Psychopathy and Abnormal Character). Münch. Med. Woch. 1926. F. Siebold: *"Erblichkeit und Psychopathie"* (Heredity and Psychopathy). Klin. Woch. 1934. H. 33. W. Bohning: *"Der schaffende Künstler und sein Werk"* (The Creative Artist and His Work). Archiv für Psychiatrie. 1924. H. 9.

34 W. Häberlin: *"Joh. Mueller's schönster Brief."* D. Med. Woch. 1936. H. 2.

35 Vorwohl. Münch. Med. Woch. 1930. H. 52.

36 Born: *"The Art of Schizophrenics."*

37 Born: *"Art and Mental Disease."* Born: *"Artistic Behavior of the Insane."* Prinzhorn: *"Bildnerei und Geisteskrankheit"* (Art and Mental Sickness). E. Kris: *"Bemerkungen zur Bildnerei der Geisteskranken"* (Notes on the Art of the Mentally Ill).

38 "Psycho-somatic relationship to gastro-intestinal diseases." Jour. o. the Am. Med Assoc. Sept. 23, 1944, No. 4, p. 225. E. Witkower: *"Über den Einfluss der Affekte auf den Gallenfluss"* (On the Influence of Affects on the Flow of Bile). Wien. Klin. Woch. 1928, H. 50.—*"Anatomische Erkrankungen aus seelischer Ursache"* (Anatomic Diseases from Psychic Causes). D. Med. Woch. 1930, H. 32.

39 H. Zweig: *"Seelische Beeinflussung somatischer Funktionen"* (Psychic Influences on Somatic Functions). Jack R. Ewett: *Psychosomatic Problems.*

40 Ernest Mach.

41 Münch. Med. Woch. 1934. H. 52.

INDEX

135